“DAMNO
GOVERNMENT

THE POLITICAL, ECONOMIC & MONEY SYSTEMS, AFTER THE DEVILS OWN HEART!

Author Wendall Dennis

ISBN 1-4120-3303-9 Cat.#04-1130-
DAM-OCRACY.NET ON THE WEB

In appreciation of, and thanks too, my American ancestors, without whose spirit, dedication, and sacrifice, my very positive life experiences would not have been possible.

I dedicate this book and my future efforts, toward the correction of the very disastrous course upon which their/our nation is now embarked, beginning with the following questions:

Would a “civilized society” purchase its security with the life blood of its youth; while, by reducing current taxes, defer the cost of the war, to the survivors of those who fought it?

What is the prognosis of a society, who will willingly sacrifice the future of its children, on the alter of perpetual debt?

How long can a nation of the people, by the people, and for the people, expect to survive, with these mind sets?

A special thanks to Robert Brevig , author of the very fine book, Beyond our Consent, for his encouragement, advise, and contribution of the Foreword.

And, as the saying goes: “Last but not least,” too my wonderful wife, companion and best friend for the last forty five years, a very resounding thank you, for your love, devotion, and long suffering. By the way, it’s just a computer , not a mistress!

Note for Librarians: a cataloguing record for this book that includes Dewey Decimal Classification and US Library of Congress numbers is available from the National Library of Canada. The complete cataloguing record can be obtained from the National Library's online database at:
www.nlc-bnc.ca/amicus/index-e.html
ISBN 1-4120-3303-9
Printed in Victoria, BC, Canada

TRAFFORD

Offices in Canada, USA, Ireland, UK and Spain
This book was published on-demand in cooperation with Trafford Publishing. On-demand publishing is a unique process and service of making a book available for retail sale to the public taking advantage of on-demand manufacturing and Internet marketing. On-demand publishing includes promotions, retail sales, manufacturing, order fulfilment, accounting and collecting
royalties on behalf of the author.
Books sales in Europe:
Trafford Publishing (UK) Ltd., Enterprise House, Wistaston Road Business Centre, Wistaston Road, Crewe CW2 7RP UNITED KINGDOM
phone 01270 251 396 (local rate 0845 230 9601)
facsimile 01270 254 983; info.uk@trafford.com
Book sales for North America and international:
Trafford Publishing, 6E–2333 Government St.,
Victoria, BC V8T 4P4 CANADA
phone 250 383 6864 (toll-free 1 888 232 4444)
fax 250 383 6804; email to bookstore@trafford.com

www.trafford.com/robots/04-1130.html

10 9 8 7 6 5 4 3 2 1

FOREWORD
By
Robert Harris Brevig

Americans entering the Twenty-first Century, need to be asking themselves why, after two-and-a-quarter centuries of freedom from the clutches of tyranny as a Constitutional Republic; the governing precepts under which our nation was founded, are we suddenly defining ourselves as a democracy?

This is a rather curious state of affairs, when given histories very damning commentary, on the inevitable fate of all established democracies.

The ideal of democracy, while on the surface has an almost universal appeal, in practice, has never been able to inspire the desired attributes necessary to its maintenance, in the people it has embraced.

The socio-political concept of democracy inevitably become its own worst enemy? Why is this so?

Let us first briefly examine how some of history's greatest minds have summarized what can be expected from a democracy, beginning with a portion of Plato's commentary on democracy, and the effects of democratic principles upon the common man's mind.

Nearly 2500 years ago, he opined:

"And when they have emptied and swept clean his soul of him who is now in their power, and who is being initiated by them in great mysteries, the next thing is to bring back to their house, insolence, anarchy, waste and impudence.

In bright array, having garlands on their heads, and a great company with them, hymning their praises and calling them by sweet names; insolence they term breeding; and anarchy, liberty; waste, magnificence, and impudence, courage.

And so the young man passes out of his original native, which was trained in the school of necessity, into the freedom and libertinism of useless and unnecessary pleasures."

These words were inspired during the final days of decadence of the Greek Empire, when democracy was in its fullest blossom.

His most famous pupil, Aristotle, had the following to say:

"If liberty and equality, as is thought by some, are chiefly to be found in democracy, they will be best attained when all persons alike, share in the government to the utmost."

Presumably this means that we will only have true democracy, when we are all employed by our governments, in the business of enforcing our edicts, against one another, since this seems to be what governments do best.

Moving on to more modern times, we find the following comments by Alexis de Tocqueville:

"He feared that the inevitable growth of democracy would also lead to despotism and militarism. While peace is particularly hurtful to democratic armies, war, and its popular passions, give them advantages, which cannot fail in the end, to give to them the victory.

The secret connection between the military character and that of democracy is the profit motive. No protracted war can fail to endanger the freedom of a democratic country. If only because it must increase the powers of civil government."

He went on to say:

"The surface of American society is covered with a layer of democratic paint, but, from time to time, one can see the old aristocratic colours breaking through."

Moving on to some of the thoughts our own forefathers and great patriots: Thomas Jefferson, the third President of the United States felt that:

"A democracy is nothing more than mob rule, where fifty-one percent of the people may take away the rights of the other forty-nine."

H. L. Mencken had this to say about democracy:

"Democracy is only a dream; it should be put in the same category as Arcadia, Santa Claus and Heaven."

Agnes Repplier said:

"Democracy forever teases us with the contrast between its ideals and its realities, between its heroic possibilities and its sorry achievements."

In the ensuing twenty-five centuries since the time our historians first noted mankind's experience with democracy, his attempts to realize this ideal have filled our history books with failures, one collapsing upon the other, like dominoes.

In the present however, we are left with two predominate concepts still vying for acceptance as the ideal form of government... the Democratic Republic and the Social Democracy.

Strangely enough, these two bastardized concepts do not seem to antagonize each other sufficiently to come to blows militarily on the battlefield, but instead spar away at each other with thickly padded gloves, in the domain of socio-economics and politics.

They do not seem to be such blood-thirsty antagonists, as are monarchical dictatorships, and inevitable aristocracies; with their elected parliaments and representative assemblies.

Yet, in all this time, there is no convincing evidence that human nature has changed sufficiently to competently embrace the spirit, of romanticized democracy.

The reader of this excellent treatise on the historical legacy of democracy, titled "DAMN-OCRACY", researched and written by Wendall Dennis, will soon realize that we humans are still in our infancy, with our relationship to the promises made by the democratic ideal.

As such, it can perhaps only be used as a weapon; a means of which we may be forced unknowingly, and without our awareness, into submission to socio-economic, and political enslavement.

Our Constitutional Fathers, familiar with the strength and weaknesses of both autocracy and democracy, with fixed principles definitely in mind, defined a Representative Republican form of government. They made a very marked distinction between a republic and a democracy--and said repeatedly and emphatically that they had founded a Republic.

Read the words that follow with great care, fellow Americans, and be on guard. Yours and your children's future liberty are in the balance.

TABLE OF CONTENTS

ABOUT THE AUTHOR

My name is Wendall Dennis; I am a seventy years old white male; born and raised Texan, now living in the Snake River valley of Idaho.

The purpose of this book is to give voice to many millions of fellow citizens, who, like me are sick and tired *of being mushroomed by our "public servants," you know, kept in the dark; fed shit; and* then dubbed "the silent majority."

Many Of Us Are Silent, Because Until The Advent Of The Internet, We Have Had No Voice!

Having chosen to make our living by providing the goods and services which keep this nation running, we have acquired our education, and gained our experience, toward the fulfillment of these obligations.

Many of us are not college educated, and are therefore, not to be mistaken as "professionals."

Being "uneducated," our opinion is neither courted, nor desired, you know: *"Just get in, Sit down, Hang on, and Shut up." We will tell you what to think, and when the time is right, for whom to vote.*

Those educated in the professions: engineers, teachers, doctors, and nurses, ad infinitum; fair no better.

Despite degrees testifying too the many years dedicated too the acquisition of knowledge, they too are assumed incapable of understanding a government supposedly created, and allegedly operating in accordance with a constitution; written by people with far less education.

A vast majority of the media representatives, the people who

have had a voice, acquired their education within a very small facet of expertise, acquiring a proficiency in what, not how to think.

They have absolutely no idea of what is involved in being a carpenter, electrician, or plumber; what it takes to be an auto mechanic; to build and maintain a fleet of airplanes; too spend endless, boring hours, looking at the world through the windshield of a truck; or to be totally immersed, day in and day out, by life and death issues, as are police and firemen.

They neither know nor care about the money, time, and hard work expended by the farmer growing the food and fiber; the gamble and prayers that the rains will come in due season, in moderation, and that the winter will hold off just one more week.

They have no basis of understanding the plight of the itinerant field hands, the oil patch roustabout, the lumberjack, the coal miner, nor textile workers, and others who work for a very small wage, putting the food on their grocery shelves, and the shirt or blouse on their backs.

My story is not unique among the working class. Most of us outside the "system" have acquired a sever skepticism, and a feeling of impotence in determining our future welfare.

Many of us recognize the fact that something is drastically wrong within the system itself, something at times manifesting as insanity within a portion of our citizenry.

Consequently, we are not insulated by wealth, or education, to the causes, and, correspondingly to the corrections, which must be implemented.

Lawful and Legal are terms which we have been very erroneously taught to think of as synonymous.

In Truth, the Citizens of This Nation are Suffering the Consequences of a Legally Constituted Government, Operating

ABOUT THE AUTHOR

Unlawfully.

The message which has been sent by those of us who have chosen not to vote, has been interpreted by the politicians as apathy, while in truth, a far more accurate assessment, is that of futility.

It is no secret, that for many years our government has been contaminated by corruption; corruption knowingly instituted by past representatives, and perpetuated by the present ones; corruption which has resulted in the transformation to the unlawful state.

Is it really so hard to understand the strongly held conviction, that a vote to either candidate, constitutes tacit approval of this legal, but unlawful system?

Instead of attempting to determine just why the system appears to be collapsing, and respect for government vanishing, many government "officials" with support of the "media," in an attempt to head off a sensed and growing demand for system reformation, are constantly trying to persuade us that the solution to all our ills, is to first criminalize ownership, and then confiscate privately held weapons.

There is however, one thing wrong with the plan! It entails declaring war on the main stream citizenry of the nation!

Citizens who have served their country, fought its wars, and built its society, in addition to its roads, houses, and businesses.

Citizens who have tilled its soil, and delivered its merchandise-- in short, people who cannot be labeled as fanatics, weirdo's, or space cadets.

Lost on these "would be rulers," is the fact, that the vast majority of we the people, are well aware, that most of our problems are not caused by our disobedience to the nations natural laws, but by our Non-Representatives disobedience to the nations

ABOUT THE AUTHOR

Supreme Law.

The increasingly pervasiveness of laws, whose sole intent is the invasion of personal privacy, and control of the individual citizen, despite what many of our government "officials" seem to think, is not going un-noticed.

We the people, in increasing numbers, having been rudely awakened by the fact that our personal economic scenario, doesn't square with the sunshine and roses political version, are looking for answers.

My Intent Is To Supply At Least A Few Of Them!

I have been the beneficiary of a very loving environment all my life. I have been married to a very loving and lovely lady for forty-five years, and we have raised four very well adjusted, and productive children.

My parents were married for over 50 years, as were my wife's, and our fathers provided an adequate, though, by no means lavish life style.

Thanks to my father, I have never known hunger, neither was I furnished a lot of superfluous items, making do with second hand bicycles, as an example.

In the late nineteen forties, at about the age of 14, I earned and saved the $43.00 required to purchase a new one, "pulling bolls" in Mr. Rays cotton patch, in Lubbock County Texas.

That's 4300 pounds of cotton at $1.00 per hundred--believe me, that qualifies as hard earned money. (anyone who has ever "pulled boles" can verify this)

Typically TEXAN, I was raised in a religious environment, and have spent many hours in church, acquiring a good understanding of the Christian Bible and faith.

ABOUT THE AUTHOR

As the result, from the early days of my youth, well into my Forties, I was very active in formal church services. I have taught Sunday School, spoken from the pulpit, and have even considered going into the ministry. However, I now consider myself Deist.

I have tried to take very good care of the health, with which my Creator honored me. I have never been drunk--have never smoked--and have never used drugs, (very seldom even aspirin), I haven't been sick, not even a cold, for the better part of fifty years.

I was an apprentice carpenter while still in high school. I have had as many as three jobs simultaneously; have served in the Infantry, and as a commissioned police officer.

I have worked in retail management, as a boat mechanic, maintenance mechanic, roofing contractor, and owner and operator of my own mobile home set up and improvement company.

In the mid sixties, while in Lubbock, I applied for work as an airplane mechanic trainee with The Boeing Airplane Co. located in Renton, Washington and was accepted. We moved to the Puget Sound area in mid 1966.

Family matters required that we return to the Southwest in 1974. In 1989, family matters resolved, my wife and I returned "home" to the Seattle area, which we love.

However, it is loved by way too many others, so, tired of fighting traffic, in 1999 my wife and I moved to the Snake River valley of Idaho.

Read the book, get mad, and then help to re-introduce a bunch of parasites, too the real world.

INTRODUCTION

I Pledge My Devotion to My God--The Flag--The Cause of Liberty--And The Nation, Dedicated by Our Forefathers; Purchased With Their Lives; And Nurtured With The Blood of Following Generations; Too The Securing of Individual Sovereignty For All.

The focus of this book is the exploration of the possibility, and the postulation of the probability, that the financial system, and the US government, as we know it, is destined to either collapse, or, at least experience massive change.

If this indeed proves to be the case, the manner and focus of its rebuilding will determine the fate of our freedom. We, the citizens of the time, must dedicate our lives to, and accept nothing less, than individual sovereignty, or learn to live in captivity!

The following book is the result of over twenty years of study and deductive reasoning. I am an avid reader, hence, there is no way that I can either recall or acknowledge the names of all the people who have influenced my thinking, in the time span of nearly seventy years.

By committing to paper, contemporary observations and conclusions based on others work, I acknowledge and honor man kinds continuing quest for the immortal, as well as clues to aid us in establishing our place in the eternal scheme.

In essence, my intent is to give credit and thanks to those whom I remember, and others whom I do not; some living, others long in the grave, for fulfilling their obligations of expanding wisdom and sharing it with me, as well as their many other descendants.

I, as well as many of my fellow citizens, have developed a sever

skepticism concerning the course upon which our nations government has embarked within the last forty years. Many of us have reached the conclusion that the "experts" whom we have relied upon to chart the course of our ship of state, could not find their butts with both hands.

The active writing has occurred whenever I could find the time after work or on weekends, and could shake the guilt trip of not acquiescing to my wife's suggestions of outings to the mountains, ocean, rivers, and other destinations of natural beauty in the Pacific Northwest.

It is my conviction, that unless I, and a large number of my fellow travelers begin to spend less time enjoying the natural beauty and recreational opportunities of our respective areas, and more time supervising and reassessing the role of our representatives to government, that very soon we will no longer be free to go where we want, and do what we please.

The atrocities in Waco, Texas, Ruby Ridge Idaho, and the recently passed "homeland security" legislation, has prompted me to spend more time, with less guilt, staring at this computer screen.

It is not my intent to be vindictive, however, each pointed finger will require that I step on the toes of some very powerful people, to call into question some strong beliefs, to rattle some long forgotten skeletons, and lay bare the foundation of our society itself.

I no doubt will become the grinch who stole Christmas, the skunk who attended the picnic in the park, and the little boy pointing out that the Emperor has no clothes, all rolled up into one.

We are literally awash in a sea of information, we have no escape from it. For anyone with a true desire to know the answer to any question, the only requirements are an open mind and the willingness to invest the necessary time reading, compiling, analyzing, and correlating this glut of information.

They must also be willing to examine, dissect, and if necessary, unlearn previous "truth." Contemporary information, preserved knowledge, and current experiences, could, and should, result in applied wisdom.

Fascination is a precursor of the desire to acquire knowledge. Because small children do not inherently recognize danger, they will attempt to touch fire, or grab a spinning saw blade, so we protect them from the consequences of ignorance.

Instinct is a reminder to the species of this debt--each of us, as beneficiaries of protective knowledge, are obligated to pass it own. Most of us assume this responsibility as soon as we recognize it, as an example: it is not uncommon for a four year old child to attempt to protect a two year old.

These instincts remain in most of us for the duration of our lives, in a few however, they seem never to have existed.

We all desire to improve our circumstances, as well as those of our community, and to have these accomplishments preserved, precluding our following generations from being required, as a current cliché expresses it, "to re-invent the wheel." This is where the obligation ends.

Records and artifacts of the knowledge exist, as well as the results of their application. It is the choice of our following generation to utilize, disregard, or to even fail to seek them out. They, as were we, are free to either reinvent the wheel, improve upon its design, or, even do without it.

As it relates to government, it seems that each generation insists upon making many of their own decisions from scratch, repeating many of the errors, and suffering the same consequences.

Through the ages, many, figuratively speaking, have insisted upon holding fire and grabbing the spinning blade, even after having been advised, through history of the danger, and observing first hand the damage suffered by others who failed to heed the warnings.

As trustees of a legacy it becomes our responsibility, if this legacy has any value to us, to seek out its history and to determine if its value is worth the price demanded of us to maintain and bequeath to following generations.

Does it require changes to make it better conform to our needs, or will changes destroy it? These are questions to which we all must seek answers.

My only desire is to hold the mirror of history for our nation, allowing the concerned among us to compare the reflections of our current problems face to face, with the problems faced by our ancestors.

We may then draw conclusions and formulate actions to be taken, utilizing lessons of the past. Without question, many of these answers will dictate change in government policy, as well as personal attitudes and life styles.

This spawns an interesting question: Do enough of us really desire the answers, or will we wait until after we, as a nation, have been required to reclaim the freedom that many of us now take for granted?

This observation springs from the fact that it has been neither easy nor pleasant for me to unlearn "ancient truth," thus, I realize that it is going to be even harder and more unpleasant for many, and even impossible, for some of my fellow citizens to accept these conclusions.

I, more than anyone, recognize my limitation of education and seeming lack of qualification, however, because many of the educated members of our society appear to be dismayed by the conditions--and the analysis of those attempting to find answers appear lacking, my hope is that my conclusions will be read, and any deserved merit added to that of the better educated.

Several year ago, when this project began, I harbored some very real doubts that what I wrote would be printed, and some very real fears of the repercussions if it were, however, I have been unable to stop writing.

I determined to fulfill what I perceived to be an obligation to travelers along this common and eternal road, and to trust my creator for its publication. If you are reading it, my trust has been rewarded.

I realize that this book is guaranteed to create an over abundance of enemies, I hope that it generates even more friends and allies, of not only myself, but of a nation in very grave peril.

We each harbor our own unique perspectives and definitions of freedom; for too long we have taken these blessings for granted. However, there exist now, as never before, a concerted effort to rob us of the right to these definitions, and to replace them with state imposed mandates.

Patrick Henry, an original patriot, recognized the fact that unless the right of self determination existed, life had no value.

A portion of the following speech, made to his fellow delegates at the founding convention in the year 1775 has been repeated by teachers to students in classrooms throughout this nation, for over two hundred years. Quote:

"Mr. President, it is natural to man to indulge in the illusions of hope. We are apt to shut our eyes against a painful truth. Is this the part of wise men, engaged in a great and arduous struggle for liberty?

Are we disposed to be of the number of those, who, having eyes , see not, and having ears, hear not, the things which so nearly concern their temporal salvation?

For my part, whatever anguish of spirit it may cost, I am willing to know the whole truth, to know the worst, and to provide for it.

I have but one lamp by which my feet are guided, and that is the lamp of experience. I know of no way of judging of the future but by the past. Let us not, I beseech you, sir, deceive ourselves longer.

Sir, we have done everything that could be done to avert the storm which is now coming on. We have petitioned; we have remonstrated; we have supplicated; we have prostrated ourselves before the throne, and have implored its interposition to arrest the tyrannical hands of the ministry and Parliament.

Our petitions have been slighted; our remonstrance's have produced additional violence and insults ; our supplications have been disregarded; and we have been spurned, with contempt, from the foot of the throne!

In vain, after these things, may we indulge the fond hope of peace and reconciliation. There is no longer any room for hope. If we wish to be free--if we mean to preserve inviolate those inestimable privileges for which we have been so long contending--if we mean not basely to abandon the noble struggle in which we have been so long engaged, and which we have pledged ourselves never to abandon, until the glorious object of our contest shall be obtained-- we must fight! I repeat it, sir we must fight! An appeal to arms and to the God of Hosts is all that is left us!

They tell us, sir, that we are weak--unable to cope with so formidable an adversary. But when shall we be stronger? Will it be the next week, or the next year? Will it be when we are totally disarmed? Shall we acquire the means of effectual resistance by lying supinely on our backs and hugging the delusive phantom of hope, until our enemies shall have bound us hand and foot?

INTRODUCTION

Sir, we are not weak if we make a proper use of those means which the God of nature has placed in our power. Three millions of people armed in the holy cause of liberty, and in such country as that which we posses, are invincible by any force which our enemy can send against us. Besides, sir, we shall not fight our battles alone. There is a just God who presides over the destines of nations, and who will raise up friends to fight our battles for us. The battle, sir, is not to the strong alone; it is to the vigilant, the active, the brave.

It is in vain, sir to extenuate the matter. Gentleman may cry "Peace, Peace"--But there is no peace. The war is actually begun! Our brethren are already in the field! Why stand we here idle? What is it that gentle-men wish? What would they have? Is life so dear, or peace so sweet, as to be purchased at the price of *chains and slavery? Forbid it, Almighty God! "I know not what course others my take, but as for me, give me liberty, or give me death."* Unquote.

The connotation of this speech, figuratively speaking became a guidon--leading generation after generation of our youth onto battlefields around the world, in an effort to aid our fellow mans struggle to attain the blessings of liberty.

Many Now Lie in Cemeteries in Foreign Lands.

From all appearances, a very large number of our current populace have either forgotten the speech, have never been exposed to it, or have written it off as no longer appropriate in our day and age.

I'm not one of them!

I am prepared, as have been many of my contemporaries, and as was the founders of our nation, to place my personal welfare in the hands of our creator.

Although I will never gain their stature, there are far worse things to aspire to than the courage displayed by George

INTRODUCTION

Washington, James Madison, Thomas Jefferson, Thomas Paine, Martin Luther King, and Medger Evers, to name just a few.

I obviously have written from the only perspective which I know, a life time of hard work, and a view from the trenches. A product of the West Texas farming community, former FFA member and Vocational Ag student, I have dragged my fair share of cotton sacks.

If I am successful in my efforts, many of you within my peer group are going to observe that "I could have written that book." You are absolutely correct.

Drawing from past experiences of myself and others, encompassing many generations, and embracing many centuries, it is nothing more than common sense comparisons of what has and hasn't worked, and why.

Higher education has been held in high regard by most of the nations citizens for a very long time. We have given credence to the credentials of education to determine our representatives of delegated authority for generations.

The troubles facing this nation today are calling these individual credentials, and the institutions from which they were obtained, to account.

It is very troubling to many of us to realize that: *if the best people, with the best education, are formulating the best policies for this nation--Then We Are In Very Deep Trouble!*

Common sense, if it ever existed, appears to have totally disappeared from the character of many of these people.

Do degrees from Harvard, Yale, Oxford etc. irrevocably destroy this attribute, or do they merely render it inoperative?

This we do know, when coupled with election to public office, they certainly engender an attitude of elitism, arrogance, and contempt for those governed.

At this time, I would like to submit the names of Bill Clinton and Al Gore, as proof positive.

Al Gore, when caught in the act of using his office phone for fund raising in direct disobedience to the law, arrogantly stated that he was bound by no controlling legal authority.

Bill Clinton, turned his last six months in office into a vacation for himself and daughter, and in his arrogance, employed the presidential 747, and the attendant support staff, planes, and cars, as his own private airline, and security personnel as personal servants.

This pomposity, in all likelihood cost the American people well in excess of one hundred million dollars.

Adding insult too injury, by callously passing out pardons in wholesale quantity, *he mocked the time, money, and dedication to justice, of our court system.*

Common sense, as well as appreciation of the trust invested in them by their fellow citizens, should be expected to trigger an ingrained decorum of personal conduct.

Such was not the case, when recently, a vacation trip jointly enjoyed by the Vice President, and a setting Justice of the Supreme Court, arrogantly, and contemptuously, compromised the integrity of both the executive, as well as the judicial departments of government.

And now some questions: Why can the English and literary trained individuals not understand how the language of the Constitution is being distorted by the "experts?"

How can math and science graduates accept the "economists" proclamations, many of which violate all rules of mathematics?

INTRODUCTION

How can anyone accept the concept of a nation, company, or family "spending themselves into prosperity?"

With all the turmoil in this nation, why are some of these Ph.D.'s not analyzing the situation with the view that perhaps we are on the wrong path?

With teachers all over the nation threatening strike, citing, among other grievances, inadequate pay, why are they not examining the reasons for the lack of the necessary funds to increase their pay?

Why are judges, lawyers, and law professors, not attempting to analyze the failure of the entire criminal justice system?

Why are our "political scientist" not taking the system apart, analyzing it piece by piece, and formulating some conclusions as to why, from all evidence, our for bearers fought to bequeath us a system no better than the one from which they escaped?

I know what you are thinking, and you are right; the fault does not belong solely to the educated class, but to every citizen within the nation. However, the educated, particularly those educated in the law; by creation, interpretation, application and enforcement of the law, as well as control of the wealth, now enjoy total command of the government.

Perhaps I have reached some wrong conclusions; I will certainly offend a lot of people; however, I am, despite my limited education, at least attempting to glean some sense from the confusion, and in the process, address the fact that:

The government that we now "enjoy," is not that founded upon the Declaration of Independence, nor created by the Constitution.

While it is evident that changes must be instituted, presently, many people are content to merely change the "expert" representatives of the system.

INTRODUCTION

A large number of citizens, and most representatives, either refuse to acknowledge, or, are incapable of discerning, evidence coursing from a system displaying every sign of self destruction.

Thus, the political, economic, and social reality-- processes not limited to the United States, are in such dynamic change and redefinition, that any term less than revolutionary, will prove to be an inappropriate description.

The Hard Truth Is: We can chant, pray and exhort God to bless America until hell freezes over, but will still not be granted a special dispensation to violate the laws of nature, and natures god: Especially Those of Mathematics and Economics!

We Enjoy the Blessings of God, Only if We Follow the Laws of God!

For most of my life, it seems that I have been possessed by a compulsion for information; consequently, one of my greatest blessings was to be raised in a nation whose greatest attribute is its dedication to the sanctity, exploration, preservation and employment of knowledge.

A nation seemingly obsessed with its existence and dissemination, regardless of its content or nature.

In my mid forties, I discovered my skill at reasoned thought. It was as though I was suddenly awakened, by a tiny beam of white light.

While attempting to locate the source, I had the sensation of being confined in a large translucent bag; the only illumination was light filtered through the brown sides of the bag.

As I peered through the tiny pin hole, I was amazed by contradictions of what I had considered truth.

I felt a twinge of apprehension, as though I could be struck down

at anytime, as punishment for acquiring an understanding of knowledge, contrary, and thus forbidden, to that which I had been taught.

During the intervening 25 years, as previously acquired secular knowledge, became a treasure trove of understanding, I discovered that much of what I accepted as truth, was really a mirror image thereof, especially as it related to religion and government.

As I gained in education, I learned of the atrocities committed in the name of Christianity.

The radical fundamentalism, and brutality, for which our leaders are vociferously condemning the Muslim religion, was at least matched by that of Judaism and Christianity; a fact of history, which no one cares to discuss, or, even admit.

It has been estimated that the "Christian" Crusades, and Inquisitions, of the Catholic Church, resulted in the death of at least fifty million, primarily Moslem people.

During The Inquisition, individuals unfortunate enough to be singled out, were drawn and quartered on racks, butchered, burned alive, skinned alive, cooked in iron maidens, and impaled by spikes sticking through the sides of containers in which they were placed, I have seen some of these items displayed in the Tower of London.

In addition too the millions killed, over one million priceless and irreplaceable books, scrolls, and papyri were destroyed when the brave knights of the Crusades burned the libraries of Cairo and Alexandria, simply because they "might" contain information contradictory to the dogma of the "Church."

These actions alone, have cost mankind hundreds of years just piecing together our fragmented history, as a replacement for that which was virtually complete and in one place.

Science too, was set back hundreds of years, as the result of punishment, death, exile, and coerced retraction of scientific principles, today recognized as truth.

It became quite clear to me, that the "Church" was not the preserver of knowledge during the "dark ages" as I had been taught, but, contrarily was its cause. Is it any wonder that religion lost its appeal?

The doctrine of Gods Love has permeated Christian teaching primarily within the last 50 years.

Although we sing the Hymn, "Give Me That Old Time Religion," none of us in the United States, and few in the world, would live under these standards.

Until very recently Dante's Inferno was the basis for many "hell fire and brimstone" sermons preached in this nation, I have listened to more than my share of them.

In my youth, the statement "That it is a fearful thing to fall into hands of the living God," was far more common, than the statement, that God is Love.

The slave ships sailed under the flag of the cross, and the Catholic Church profited from the sale of their cargo.

Rather than help free the black race, Christian Churches taught, and preached, inferiority and segregation, IN MY LIFETIME.

The KKK came out of the Southern Christian congregations, and helped keep the black population down after the Civil War, and is active even today.

It stands to reason that if the vestiges of our material world require good foundations, then the foundations upon which our spirituality is based, is even more crucial.

Although the cathedrals, and churches are built upon strong

foundations, religious doctrines, until very recently, were constructed almost entirely upon institutionalized bigotry, racism, and elitism.

In addition, even a cursory look at the Book of Genesis, the very the beginning of the Bible, reveals a very flawed view of how the solar system works.

If this is a revelation of God, then why was humankind, the entity created In The Image and After the Likeness of the Supreme Being, misled?

If I cannot trust the accuracy of the first few sentences of an "inspired book" why should I accept the rest at face value? For this reason, I now demand verification, thus my departure from the edifices of organized religion.

Through my experience, I have discovered the difficulty involved in unlearning "truth;" many find it impossible, while others are unwilling to even subject their "truth" to the test.

Religion and government have forever been joined at the hip, with constantly changing artificial laws made to comply with the contrived and constantly changing versions of religion, the effect has been governments constructed and working at cross purposes with the truth.

Thus I began studying the Declaration of Independence--creating a government in which every person within the nation was sovereign, and every person on the globe, deserving of the opportunity of at least attempting to be self determining.

One question began to nag at me: If this is a Christian nation as claimed, then why was the Declaration of Independence dedicated to the Laws of Nature and Natures God?

We know for a fact that Thomas Jefferson and all the co-signers of the document were certainly familiar with the Laws of Jehovah and Jehovah God?

INTRODUCTION

In My "Eureka" Moment, the uniqueness of The United States, a nation devoted to the absolute sanctity, thus interpretation and preservation of knowledge, as well as scientific exploration and application of the resultant discoveries, dawned on me.

Because the laws of nature, and natures God are absolutely stable, within the two century history of the US, through the understanding, preservation, distribution, magnification and adherence to these laws, mankind has developed the ability of:

Flight; making possible our physical presence at locations around the globe, within hours--not days, months, or years:

World wide, instantaneous as well as simultaneous, video/ audio communications:

Instantaneous translations of language:

An understanding and mapping of our human bodies:

Launching vehicles capable of transmitting images of other worlds; controlling them from earth; and viewing the results, in the comfort of our homes:

And We Have Barely Scratched The Surface Of Our Potential!

For the first time in human history, a government free of religious dogma, thus, a representative cross section of the world, was free to embrace every race, creed, religion and nationality, in a Nation United under Common Language, <u>Not Common Religion!</u>

Quite a contradiction to the story of the tower of Babel, in which communication, and interaction between races is not permitted, and the destruction of opposing knowledge and even humanity, an article of faith.

Under this criteria, the United States, a nation in which each individual was guaranteed the freedom to devise their own unique perspective of God, or, to reject the concept entirely, is an abomination; thus, the prayer for God to bless America, would amount too an exercise in futility.

Many times I have been admonished from the pulpit, to acquiesce too the biblical concept, of obeying those with the rule over me; contrarily, the Declaration of Independence declares that I am to be governed by my consent, and that no one enjoys the right of rule over me.

As we are all familiar, the fate of this declaration of individual sovereignty, was to be decided by the successful conclusion of war.

Hooray! A sovereign people really did have the right to form a sovereign government, a government subservient to the people!

Or Did They? Were They Really Sovereign?

How was it possible for a bunch of back sliding Christians, overthrowing an established Christian government, and usurpating the role of Sovereignty, to establish Another Christian Government, as its replacement?

If You Believe The Bible: It Was Not Possible!

Our nations founders, by overthrowing an established government, a Monarchy, ruled by a Christian King, his Coronation officiated at by priest ordained by the Church, acted in direct disobedience to the admonition to: obey those with the rule over you; thus sinfully establishing the United States government.

Our nations founding documents, specifically bans royalty and aristocracy, yet the Catholic Church, the corner stone of the Christianity of the time, is organized around the biblical concept of royalty, elitism, and aristocracy.

It, as well as the Anglican Church, still preside at their Coronations.

Accordingly, If This Is Truly A Christian Nation, the only means by which it may regain its legitimacy, and be returned to the fold, is for we, the current citizens, too renounce our founders actions, and again accept the rule of the British crown, thereby repenting from their sin!

Sounds ridiculous doesn't it? And yet this is the means prescribed by the Christian Bible.

Additionally, because it contravenes the principle of perfection, it's an impossibility for a human being to enter this world by the method specifically devised by a perfect being, For That Purpose, too be conceived in sin, and born in iniquity.

Absent the supposed fall, mankind has never been in need of a rescuing priesthood.

As proven by nature, an entity must be governed by either instinct, or the capability, as well as the opportunity, of acquiring, processing, and acting upon knowledge.

The Eagle Was Not Given Wings; Then Denied Their Use!

Thus, if mankind, shorn of instinct, fell from the grace of our Creator as the result of "unlawfully" utilizing our ability of acquiring knowledge, then by what mode was mankind to live, move and have our being?

The parable of the talents in the bible itself, demonstrates that to fail to utilize entrusted abilities, is to invite the scorn of the Creator.

We each possess demonstrated talents of reasoned thought and self government, their only source was our creator.

If they were not to be utilized, what was the purpose of their bestowment?

If you believe the passages declaring God to be the same yesterday, today, and forever, and that he is no respecter of persons, then please explain to me, the existence of a "chosen people," and varying dispensations of time.

If at death, "the body returns to the earth from which it came and the spirit returns to God who gave it," as stated within the Bible, then what is there to resurrect?

In keeping with the admonition to study to show myself approved, while I do not possess the right to do wrong, I do possess the right to be wrong, in my search of the truth.

Thus, I realized that I must choose the truth as expressed within the Declaration of Independence, or, the truth as declared by various versions, factions, spokesmen, and apologist of an extremely fragmented religious organization.

I reasoned that a God either unwilling or incapable of protecting writings by which I would be judged, was not a God in which I was willing to place my trust. The words of Thomas Jefferson, and the laws of nature, made far better sense.

What I have written sheds light on my philosophical thought, which in turn flavors every syllable, of every word, which proceeds from my hand, and is important in each readers judgment of my work.

I can reveal my religious proclivities, without detailing by chapter and verse where they may be found, in a book, which, due to various translations and pomposity, I hold in varying degrees of relevance.

It is not my purpose to convert anyone to my religious persuasion, in fact, religious commentary was included, only because it is the driving force of our very being, and is impossible to eliminate from any meaningful dissertation.

Religion is a very personal choice, and I care not how anyone thinks, so long as they do not try have those beliefs applied to me, by force of law.

I am very cognizant of my fallibility, thus, any criticism of your beliefs, is only an explanation as to why they are wrong for me, not why they are wrong for you.

Absent the Freedom of Thought and Action, Life is Without Purpose!

"DAMN-OCRACY"

GOVERNMENT FROM HELL

The Political, Economic, & Money System, After The Devils Own Heart!

"Allow me to Issue and Control a Nations Money, and I Care Not Who Writes its Laws!"

This statement, attributed to Mayer Amschel Rothschild, architect of the British monetary system, was merely a recognition of the seemingly eternal reality of human bondage to the money changers.

Paraphrasing: Allow me to control the wealth of a business, home, church, or individual, and I control their Destiny!

Although Mr. Rothschild's statement dates to the late eighteenth century, those familiar with the Christian religion, are aware of the incident in the Temple between Christ and the Money Changers, when, for the only time in his life, of which we have record, he displayed the emotion of rage!

How and why the Rothschild "Dollar," (federal reserve note) was foisted upon the American people; the damage it has done our Republic: and the prospects of our escaping it, is the focus of this book; beginning with the following challenge!

If any Republi/Crat, in the current "Damn-ocratic" government, has any secret plan for the extrication of our collective asses from the clutches of this debt monster, while constantly increasing its food supply, Now Is The Time Too Unveil It!

DAMN-OCRACY OVERVIEW:

The interchangeable terms Damn-ocracy/Dam-ocracy-- Damn-ocratic/Dam-ocratic and Damn-ocrat/Dam-ocrat; when used in

this book as terms best supportive of my contentions, are defined as follows: Any form of government, encompassing Any economic system, staffed by Any individual, too which, or to whom, the descriptions or contentions, are appropriate!

The American Republic Was Purchased By, and Maintained With, the Blood of Patriots!

American Democracy was Purchased with Corporate Welfare, & Domestic Socialism!

American "Damn-ocracy", When "Paid For" With our Following Generations Future!

"Damn-ocracy.com," When Government Became a Business, With Washington DC Its Brothel!

The founders of our nation were well aware of the fact that direct democracy, as the result of politicians penchant for purchasing re-election with "gifts" from the national treasury, always transitions into "Damn-ocracy!"

With passage of the Federal Reserve Act, Mayer Rothschild's dream materialized, and is currently manifesting as the United States "Damn-ocratic" Nightmare!

The "Fed" became law the day before Christmas Eve, in the year 1913, and shortly afterwards, the German International bankers, Kuhn, Loeb and Co. an affiliate of the Rothschild's, sent one of their partners as its first director. (from Congressional Record, 1934)

Thus the stage was set for the demise of Constitutional money, to be replaced with the Rothschild "Dollar." (Federal Reserve Note)

In the early seventies, I developed a sense of foreboding about our nation, and really didn't understand why.

I had a good job with the Boeing Company, I and my family were healthy and happy, we were living in, and enjoying one of the most beautiful and prosperous places on earth, but something just wasn't right.

Call it paranoia if you like, but at any given time, this gut feeling is shared by many people within this nation, and many, like me, are convinced that we must do everything within our power to save our nation.

While in search of answers, upon encountering and analyzing the amazing circumstances surrounding the founding of this nation, I discerned what seems to me, a long term, well executed plan.

A look at history reveals that every major category of people have at one time, enjoyed a brief period of "their place in the sun," beginning with the Negro, at the dawn of civilization.

It is also true, that in the past, every possible form of government, has, at one time or another, enjoyed a successful, prosperous, and influential reign; it thus required no stretch of the imagination too deduce that: At any given time, at some place upon earth, the government required for man kinds next major evolutionary leap will exist, with the nation in which it develops, evolving into preeminence in world affairs.

The fact that evolution has resulted in the collapse, or restructuring of every government in our history, extending into the mist of antiquity, makes it quite safe to conclude, that having exhausted its resources, thus reaching the limits of its viability, the current American system is facing total restructure.

How Can I Make This Statement?

The result of a 25 years plus study of the government and religious structure of the United States, leaves no doubt in my mind, that this nation was created for the express purpose of establishing the foundation of a new era in human evolution.

The evidence, beginning with the circumstances of its birth, continuing development, prosperity, protection and prominence, all mesh too harmoniously to be mere coincidence.

A few of the many examples include: Washington's visions; the mysterious visitor urging the signing of the Declaration of Independence; the uncovering of Benedict Arnold's betrayal; the French alliance, and the presence of their fleet in New York Harbor, at precisely the opportune moment; a land mass totally stocked with everything required to not only survive, but prosper; and an indigenous population, not technologically advanced beyond the stone age.

How Have We Arrived At This Defining Moment?

The explanation begins with the fact that commencing in 1865, we have been living under a bastardized system of government, comprised of elements of the Constitution, and the British Law of the Admiralty; (captains sovereignty at sea) in short, "Damn-ocracy!"

Until the American Revolution, the accepted dictum, enforced by government, declared that the natural order of things, was for all wealth too be owned and controlled by a very small, elite segment of the population, (a landed gentry) with the right to exploit, and the duty too care for the inferior class.

Contrarily, the American philosophy stated,(in principle) that wealth, in any quantity belonged too those who either produced, or, facilitated its production, with no one bound, except by personal choice, with the duty of assisting another. (No one possessed an innate claim, too wealth produced by another.)

The purpose of American government, was the maintenance of conditions conducive too the enjoyment of the rights to life, liberty and the pursuit of happiness, too the benefit of all men.

As proclaimed, within the Declaration of Independence; two

diametrically opposed philosophies.

The fly in the ointment however, was the definition accorded the term, "men." Had the term been rendered "mankind" the all inclusive species interpretation, rather than "man," the biblically exclusive gender interpretation, the world would be a different place today.

Although Great Britain, at the conclusion of the War for Independence, lost political control of the colonies, she maintained a strong business influence.

Additionally, former subjects whose loyalty remained with the monarchy, but had resisted the impulse to move to Canada following the war, clandestinely instituted a campaign of subversion against the fledgling government.

Following the Civil War, a war which Great Britain had a strong hand in fomenting, she was successful in gaining de-facto control of the United States.

By selectively financing the bankrupt economy, the British Financial System was introduced, gradually acquiring what amounted to perpetual mortgages on the American economy, as well as a strong influence, if not control of the political system.

As the result of methodical subversion, encompassing a period of about a century and a half, privileges have been substituted for many of the original Constitutional rights.

As a result, "our" Republican system of limited government, now more closely resembles the more intrusive English Parliamentary system.

In addition, an English style, elitist dominated social structure, with over ninety percent of the real wealth, controlled by about one percent of the population, ala Great Britain, is the reality of our time.

The desire of an Englishman by the name of Cecil Rhodes, was British dominated world government, this bit of information is well known.

To this end, he instituted a system, and bequeathed his fortune, to the perpetuation of an educational system dedicated too the goal of transforming the dream into reality.

As the result, recipients of Rhodes Scholarships have acquired position of tremendous influence within the US, including business, education, and government, even attaining the Presidency.

Remember the Slogan: "The Business of America, Is Business!" Corporate Business That Is.

Since the federal government assumed control of the American school curriculum fifty years ago, beginning in the very early grades and extending into the highest level of the universities, we have been totally immersed in the British System of Corporate Business, Corporate Finance, Corporate Government, and Corporate Equity Law, the basis of all MBA, and Law degrees.

American ingenuity, productivity, resourcefulness, military might, and inherently worthless "money" has fulfilled Rhodes dream beyond his wildest expectation.

It has also created a world wide army, of semi-destitute people, people who have been exposed to a better way of life.

Anyone who believes the attempted propagation of the present elitist monetary system thus, denial of their opportunity of reaching for the stars, will be tolerated, is living in a fantasy world.

Why the term "inherently worthless money?" Anything to be money, must itself have worth, or represent something that does! True money must maintain a stable value.

There is nothing wrong with money based on assets, so long as the asset base remains stable or increases, and the money itself, remains unencumbered by debt. However, when the base of the "money" itself is debt, it is fraud, not money.

Absent the politician, currency manipulation is, and has always been viewed as counterfeiting, a crime against the dignity of the nation, and its citizenry.

In Archimedes day, it was accomplished by adulterating a nations gold coinage with base metal--in our day, the politicians didn't even bother adulterating the gold coinage, they simply confiscated it with law, and by "fiat," replaced it with paper.

Because the stealing of real money, gold and silver, from the productive element of the population is immediately and simultaneously noticed and resisted, before the Rothschild Economic\Money System could be imposed upon the United States, the destruction of the Constitutional system of commodity money was absolutely imperative.

The political redistribution of domestically created wealth, by the industrious portion of the population, to those not so inclined, has however, always offered problems.

"Damn-ocracy" To The Rescue!

The devious leaders, with promises, acquire the constituency of those who enjoy the "good life," but, for various reasons, are either incapable, or unwilling, to expend the effort necessary too provide the means.

Unlike Hitler's methods of taking the wealth, and immediately killing the unfortunate soul who happened to possess it, Promises Engender Beneficiaries!

In the United States, long term, unsustainable promises, translates as beneficiaries numbering into the Multi-Millions, just within the Senior Population!

The fulfillment of those promises, by "legally" confiscating a portion of the wealth produced by those both willing, and able, is, as previously stated, both resented and resisted.

The system then takes on the need of enforcers; people, who themselves, are willing to become their fellow citizens keepers; to be trained in the methods--render unquestioned obedience to the system--and utilize that training too either intimidate or "persuade" those unwilling to render obedience to the "law."

Thus, by unlawfully compromising the sovereignty of their fellow citizens, they destroy their own, as well as that of their family members.

That which is "illegal" for the individual, is suddenly correct policy when done in the name of the collective, with the enforcement cost paid from the "public" treasury.

Add the cost of training, equipment, support, and administration to the equation, as well as the increasing ranks of the unproductive, those with the desire to work, but, hindered in our efforts by government policy. *As an example: Intentionally increasing unemployment, for the purpose of fighting "inflation,"* and the answer reveals the seeds of eventual self destruction, a fate facing Great Britain throughout most of the 18th century.

Its roots trace directly too the corporation. The creation of Elizabeth 1 in the year 1600, as her contribution to a consortium of citizens engaged in the shipping business, it expanded the shield of Sovereign Immunity to the private business sector.

This Royal protection, "limited" the liability of investors to the amount of resources risked in the venture, with profits shielded from normal taxation, thus, the birth and inauguration of Corporate Government.

DAMN-OCRACY OVERVIEW

Under the Magna Carta, each citizen acquired responsibility, as well as protection, commensurate with their respective position within the society; much of the protection was negated.

Elizabethl, by creating a government favored business class, ushered in and era of grossly unfair competition with which cottage industry, (mom and pop) were forced to contend.

In need of cheap labor, many men awakened at sea, at the mercy of captains acting under laws of the Admiralty, the victim of press gangs--their families left to fend for themselves, with collusion of the government.

Elizabeth betrayed her subjects to enhance her wealth, in essence, through conflict of interest, selling private business, a lease on the throne.

In order to accommodate and facilitate this new "business arrangement," laws were passed making it virtually impossible for the lower classes to even feed themselves.

The prisons filled to capacity, requiring ships to be anchored in the Themes river to accommodate the overflow.

Over a period of several years, these ships, laden with their human cargo, regularly put to sea.

The "criminals" who survived inhumane conditions so brutal, that it brought tears to my eyes just reading about them, became the population of Australia. (If you have a strong stomach, read the book, Fatal Shore)

You will acquire a real understanding and admiration for the hearty Australian population, and an absolute loathing of British aristocracy!

Those in Great Britain who were not yet criminals, developed a strong desire to migrate to America, with the opportunity to create living conditions more in keeping with their natural status as free human beings, rather than servants to an aristocracy, they however were still on the kings leash.

In 1913, history repeats itself. Private business, through the Federal Reserve Corporation, "Fed" acquired a seat at the American throne, and *the corporate structure acquired the sovereignty taken from the individual citizen, at the conclusion of the Civil War.*

Sovereignty Has Its Benefits!

Accordingly, laws again were enacted favoring law and currency manipulation, at the expense of the former sovereign citizens.

Over time, the corporate structure again consolidates control of the wealth; laws again rob those citizens not prepared through training or resources to protect themselves; incarceration again becomes a growth industry, and the truism "those who do not learn from history are bound to repeat it," is again verified.

Great Britain, at the time of her crisis, had the luxury of shipping the "problem" to two distant continents, that luxury is now non-existent.

Following a short reprieve, purchased by transporting the financial burden to citizens of the future, rather than the bodies of current citizens to distant lands, We Are Destined To Ride The Back Of This Tiger To Its Lair.

Banks, insurance companies, and industrial conglomerates, have congealed into ever larger behemoths, shifting ever more control away from the citizenry, and toward government, corporations, and the Federal Reserve; a recipe for disaster.

While these three monsters are currently benefiting, they are laying the foundation for their own demise.

A bad thing? Lets look at the facts.

Our nation, as founded, wasn't dependent upon government!

It was founded as a co-operative, with citizen helping citizen, and government merely coordinating the activities.

We established an electrical grid, telephone network, roads, food and fiber production, with neighbor helping neighbor plant, harvest and transport each others produce, as well as in the construction of each others houses and barns.

Although the corporate foundation was laid in 1865, strong anti-monopolistic sentiment in Congress, stunted its growth until about 1965. (Remember President Eisenhower's warnings concerning the military industrial complex.)

We have gained immensely from the technological boom, however, the deeper we have gotten into the faceless, legalistic, wealth driven, corporate socialism, and away from the friendly cooperative, the more dysfunctional our society has become, germinating the seed of destruction of both corporate government and corporate finance.

The Federal Reserve, (created as a government servant) by stabilizing our currency, has proven a mixed blessing.

As a universal currency, it has proven very instrumental in raising the living standard in virtually every nation, it has however, robbed the American people of the control of our government.

Its ascendancy too currency of account in world trade, has swamped the United States in investment capital.

This investment frenzy has greatly distorted our domestic economy; corrupted our national values; and debauched our political system.

DAMN-OCRACY OVERVIEW

Our government is rapidly becoming superfluous; too wasteful; too expensive, and in the initial stages of deadlock.

From all indications, our military establishment, is the sole department of government working properly.

The debacle of NRON, and GLOBAL CROSSING unfolded in our living rooms, however, these companies financial problems were merely the opening act.

Remember, corporations, as derivatives of government, inherit the parental attribute of lack of imposed responsibility; while duplicating policies, practices and procedures.

The main event, entitled Financial Debacle US Government/ Federal Reserve, opens its command performance, perhaps in 2005, however, no later than 2006.

If pushed, the politicians will admit a debt of seven trillion dollars, however, with "off budget" items included, strong evidence suggests a figure closer to twenty trillion, and growing daily.

The latest estimated aggregate debt, (government and private) is in excess of Forty Trillion!

In forty years, "governed" by the Republican and Democratic Parties, our "Damn-ocracy" <u>Transitioned From Surplus</u>: Through--Hundreds of Millions-- Hundreds of Billions- Into Double Digit Trillions--of Dollars of Debt!

WHY and HOW?

SIMPLY STATED: Legality, Political Malfeasance, Criminal Irresponsibility, and Perjured Oaths, now saturate the government.

Laws which should have been declared unconstitutional were side stepped and allowed to stand, simply because it

represented a challenge too large for the Supreme Court to tackle, or was necessary to grow "Our Damn-ocracy."

Laws were fragmented, with some parts declared unconstitutional, while other parts were allowed to stand.

This obviously created incoherent legality, as evidenced by a legal system so contradictory in nature, that it is capable of supporting an army of well paid lawyers.

Legal Replaced Lawful; Relative Replaced Absolute; Equity Replaced Justice; and Bureaucratic Policy, Replaced Constitutional Law.

Thus Denied Navigational Aids, it Was Inevitable That Our "Damn-ocratic" Ship of State, Would Eventually Become Mired in the Sewer.

As you may recall, in the mid nineteen sixties, at the beginning of this nightmare, President Johnson made the statement that: "We have set in motion, forces which no one understands."

He was wrong, as represented by the following.

When I was a young lad working as a carpenter helper for my father, he asked me if I would agree to work for 31 days and accept as pay, one penny my first day, and double it each day thereafter, for the entire thirty-one day period; I of course declined, he then did the math.

Perhaps the President of the United States didn't understand the power of the exponential, but my father did, and provided me with a demonstration which I have not forgotten.

Although this power was unleashed within the United States economic system in 1913, this doomsday machine more or less slumbered until Lyndon Johnson created his "Great Society, fought a hot war in Viet Nam, and a cold one with the USSR, all on credit.

The problem intensifies! As many are aware, during the Carter administration, inflation was on the increase, it was one of the factors costing him re-election.

When Reagan assumed control, nothing affecting the true rate of inflation changed.

This is true, because the factor determining the rate of inflation, is the cost of government, the factor which he not only did not reduce, but escalated!

The focus of his policies was a decrease in taxes, and the indexing of entitlement program increases to the rate of inflation, as determined by the government.

While the economy, as the result of an invigorated business activity, itself, fueled primarily by massive increases in military procurement programs, registered a marginal increase, government debt increased at a much faster rate.

With inflation indexed to entitlements, both he, and Congress, very cognizant of the repercussions should the true inflation rate be known, escalated the policy of increasing the national debt, thereby financing *"prosperity;"* the policy which has existed to this day.

Thus, inflationary debt, (deferred taxation) is now impounded like water behind a dam, and like the water, if the dam breaks, nothing will prevent it from seeking its natural level.

It Gets Worse!

The masking of the truth, acted as restraints upon wage demands. Thus, we, the nations labor force, by not demanding wages commensurate with the true rate of inflation, are facing a wall of debt, with wages insufficient to even cover current expenses.

Compounding the problem, a large segment of the labor force, will become eligible to begin drawing Social Security benefits within ten years. The initial trickle, will, within another ten years, become an unremitting flood, thus, while disbursement escalates, income recedes.

The only means of honoring trillions of dollars in promises, is through the inflation of the currency; a process which must begin immediately.

However, the indexing of entitlement cost of living increases, to the rate of inflation, translates as disaster for the Federal Reserve, the entity responsible for funding not only Social Security, but all other entitlement programs.

The chickens of irresponsibility know their way home, and are now returning to the roost.

The trustees of the Social Security system, very cognizant of this fact, are warning that the system will be in deep trouble beginning in 2015, this is a very optimistic projection.

When repercussions from the destruction of a profitable labor force; *(unemployment disbursements replace tax revenues)* and the shock waves yet to be felt from the Trade Center, and stock market disasters, are factored into the equation, the result is economic chaos long before 2015.

Further complicating the problem, is the fact that the debt machine is now concentrating control of the wealth so rapidly, that it is threatening to suck the vast majority of the purchasing power, out of the Anglo world economy.

By hiding inflation, in the form of debt, this compound interest machine, is, in a sense, cannibalizing itself.

Lost in translation, is the fact that commerce is composed of two parts. First must be product creation, or a willingness of someone to perform a service.

Second is the peddling of either the goods or services; in a word, brokerage, and transport.

As we are all aware, this second step, especially in a global economy, actually consist of numerous steps, each adding to the eventual price.

No problem, if the fair market value, is an accumulative of fair market cost at every step.

If the creator of the product, or, provider of a service is initially short changed, over time, if the medium of exchange is honest money, market forces will equalize, and the problem will resolve itself. (supply and demand)

However, at the point in time that another participant, although adding no value to the transaction, is allowed to profit by arbitrarily determining the "value" of the "money" natural market forces cease to function, and fraud runs rampant. (current US, as well as world situation)

Thus, when this third aspect of commerce is inserted into the mix, especially when it provides representatives of government a simple and inconspicuous means of escaping the natural chains of responsibility "Damn-ocracy," the government from hell, will have been unloosed within the nation.

It is at that point, inevitable, and only a matter of time, until legitimate commerce ceases to function, yet the tainted "money" continues to enrich its owners, devouring government, business, and personal resources, in prodigious quantities!

The Foundation For These Eventualities ,Was Laid By The US Congress, In December, 1913. **(Commandeered Dollar Ch.)**

Thus, for ninety years the Federal Reserve/Federal Government books have been "cooked" into many different recipes; the chefs

congratulated with raises, bonuses, and job retention; and the occasional bout of indigestion, successfully treated, by sending the problem to the next generation.

That Next Generation Is Us!

Although common sense was shouting that there was something wrong with this picture, it was certainly in no politicians best interest, to acknowledge the impoverished pantry.

Following years of successfully "hiding" inflation in plain slight, and then denying its existence, seemingly we are now faced with the choice of either major depression, or major inflation.

From the bankers view, the clear choice would appear obvious, save what you can! Print More Money!

Although the money may be worth less, the banking system is better served with an abundance of cash, than an over abundance of uncollectable debt.

However, because the resultant inflation, translates into massive increases in the cost of entitlements, in any eventuality, The Federal Reserve is facing "the devil and the deep blue sea scenario. A vicious cycle, self engineered!

Alan Greenspan, President Bush, and the Congress, now facing essentially the scenario that I have just presented, must devise a means of funding, and distributing, fifty years of inflation, which, according too the government, does not exist: Without breaking the Dam!

Inflation is only one barb on this hook, taxation of labor is the other!

Time, The Ultimate Capital!

Because it is irreplaceable, the most valuable possession of any individual is time, once gone, gone for good.

The foundation of our nation was based upon this fact, and was provided for within the Constitution, as is the plan, for the Lawful funding, of the Lawful expenses, of the federal government.

It was recognized by our nations founders, that anything, except food, clothing, and shelter, for which a person exchanges a portion of their time, is of less value than the time itself.

Thus, the LAWFUL economic base of the nation, as established by the original Constitutional Convention, written into the Supreme Law of the Land, and Ratified by Every State, has always been gold and silver; commodity money, itself possessing intrinsic value.

The realization that the exchange of labor, for the lawful money of the land, (gold and silver) constituted barter, not income, was reflected by the prohibition of direct taxation of the individual.

Congress committed a criminal act against the American People by abolishing gold and silver coinage, *in the absence of a Constitutional Amendment*.

Compounding the offense with perjured oaths, our government "representatives," by enacting an income tax, did so, again, in direct contradiction to, and in complete disregard of, the Constitution.

Our lower court system, by upholding legislation with full knowledge that it was purposely written with the intent to defraud, aided and abetted the financial rape of the American people.

The Supreme Court, with their ruling that the 16th Amendment, conferred no new taxing authority, confirms this statement.

So while the government was intentionally misleading We The People concerning inflation, they were also unlawfully taxing,

the already deficient return on labor, thus depriving the work force, the foundation of the nation itself, of a sound financial base, forcing us into the waiting arms of the currency manipulators.

Absent an amendment, Congress, powerless to declare anything else as money, shackled the American citizenry with Rothschild "Dollars," and delivered us thus bound, to begin an eternal sentence of slavery to the international bankers.

As an aid in the harvest of the wealth, the Internal Revenue Service was instituted, and in the absence of any provision within the Constitution with which to enforce the income tax code, tax courts were established, essentially instituting the debtors prison system, the system from which our nations founders had rebelled.

An Individual Born Into Debt, Is Not Born Free!

Purchased with the blood of our forefathers, and defended with the blood of following generations, what was to be gained in 1913, that would induce a faction within our elected government, including the President, to deliver a nation so purchased, into perpetual slavery to the money changers?

Can anyone think of any justification for a government, with taxing authority, to consistently borrow operating revenue, pay interest on the borrowed money, and then utilize that authority to merely pay that interest, thus encumbering our freedom, and jeopardizing our following generations future, with unpayable debt?

Perhaps a Far More Pertinent Question Is: From 1913 to the present, what has induced the tens of thousands of our fellow citizens, having been honored with the same trust, and having uttered the same oath, to perpetuate this betrayal for an additional ninety years?

These Senators, Congress People, Presidents and Judges,

forgetting from whence they were chosen, have turned deaf ears and blind eyes to the concerns of millions of common folk, as we the unrepresented people, have attempted to address the injustices through proper channels!

So, for over fifty years, as *we the working people,* by the millions, are unjustly accused, tried, bankrupted, and imprisoned, rather than abolish the treasonous legislation, our non-representatives have devoted their time toward the enhancement of escape clauses within the tax code, too the benefit of multinational corporations.

Meanwhile, with a tax code in constant flux, and daily becoming more heinous, they relentlessly tighten the noose around the neck of *we the common people*, unincorporated business, and state government.

Administration of this god awful system, not only devours our hours by the millions, and our wealth by the billions, as an agency authorized by Congress, with approval of the courts, to act outside the restraints of the Constitution, "tax time" fosters untold consternation among most of us, and abject terror among others.

The problems now facing the citizenry of California, although the first and most conspicuous, are merely harbingers of that facing not only every state, but the federal government.

Thus our "Public Servants" contribution to our "welfare" is an impending depression, the result of ninety years of fraud.

How may the unlawfully confiscated economic base, be expeditiously returned to the states and citizenry?

Obviously It Can't!

Wealth which should have been utilized to immediately, and fully fund the Federal Government, for years has instead been utilized to set the stage for the day when the cost of deceptive postponement, and reality, would meet, face to face.

That Day Has Arrived!

Although the full impact of this theft is perhaps a couple of years away, and the economic rape of the work force will perhaps never be officially admitted, the quandary posed by this question is now taunting the administration, as reflected by tax credits and refunds.

However, considering the enormity of the problem, that approach is nothing more than an exercise in futility, much too little, and far too late!

Compared to funds required to revitalize the basic economy, it's akin to attempting to fill the Grand Canyon, a table spoon of sand at a time.

Untold Trillions of dollars of aggregate debt, cannot be recovered by paying less tax, while increasing government spending, regardless of how the concept is packaged and presented.

While our national debt represents un-printed currency, our balance of payment deficit represents money which should have been created and put into the hands of those creating the wealth.

Justifying it with the philosophy, of " O well, they are living under a different monetary system, and do not really need a better wage," the corporate system, by shorting the wages of foreign workers, while impoverishing our domestic work force, has simultaneous destroyed the customer base required to correct our trade imbalance.

In the long run, "corporate business," by not fairly compensating the craftsmen of other nations, cripple their tax base; the American people, through "foreign aid," then contribute too the support of their government.

Thus we, the tax payers, finance the transference of our employment opportunities, while corporate government, and corporate business, in tandem, preside over the destruction of our nations economic base.

Many of us, having invested our trust, and devoted our lives to various corporate business enterprises, are now being rudely awakened by this aristocratic reality of corporate philosophy:" The purpose of labor, is the enrichment of management; the personal time and welfare of the" lower class" is of no importance."

This buy cheap, sell dear philosophy, taken to the extreme, and encouraged by government tax policy, is now in the process of devastating market place, as well as work place USA.

Rothschild "Dollars" that seemingly flowed in torrents three years ago, are becoming scarce, and, from office manager to CEO, as unemployment sweeps the nation, "management" is being rudely awakened by the realization that their "positions" are merely another division of labor.

Teachers in virtually every state are threatening strikes, only to find themselves staring into empty treasuries.

Foreclosures and bankruptcies, already epidemic, as yet are only hinting at what is in store, as repercussions from the theft of the economic base, unabatedly continues the devastation of every state economy.

In its proper sequence, money is a derivative of tangible wealth, however, for the last ninety years, the monetary structure has favored those reaping huge profits by the manipulation of the laws and currency, while intentionally "shorting" the money supply to the producers of wealth, for the purpose of "fighting inflation."

Wealth in Oct. 1929, at the outset of the last depression, was very sparsely enjoyed, primarily because then, as now, the money

supply was introduced into circulation from the top, and allowed to "trickle down" to the working population.

A very large percentage of the families, especially rural families, lived at just above the subsistence level, and the nations farmers, while producing the nations food and fiber, depended upon the "generosity" of the banker to even keep his land.

This same cycle of events, following the same scenario, is now in the process of being played out world wide!

Today however, wealth, although mortgaged to the hilt, is represented by cars, boats, real estate, etc. and a higher standard of living.

This wealth, as well as the living standard, is enjoyed by most of the population, a population with a strong sense of entitlement.

The few people who believe that these possessions and aspirations will be easily relinquished, as were farms in the last depression, are in for a very rude awakening.

While the number of potentially affected citizens has increased arithmetically, our level of patience has decreased geometrically. Translation: *Larger bomb, shorter fuse.*

I Reiterate!

If any Republi-Crat in the current "Damn-ocratic" government, has any secret plan for the extraction of our collectives asses from the clutches of the debt monster, while constantly increasing its food supply, now is the time to unveil it!

In the meantime, I would like to call the following statement, too the attention of our Non-Representatives!

"When a long train of abuses and usurpations, pursuing invariably the same Object, evinces a design to reduce them

under absolute Despotism, it is their right, it is their duty, to throw off such government, and to provide new Guards for their future security."

This was a small portion of the statement known as the Declaration of Independence, a document with which many of you, our Non-Representatives are apparently unfamiliar.

Just as the wages of sin is death, according to the above passage, so also are the wages of unlawful government. I would suggest that you take the time to study that document in its entirety!

As the disappearance of government organizations, purchased painstakingly over many years appears more likely, some super wealthy power manipulators, are contemplating the prospects of watching enormous wealth, disappear like a house of cards in a Texas twister, right along with a brothel full of prostitutes, currently masquerading as "public servants."

We, very shortly, are too be presented with the opportunity to really re-invent government, by returning to basics.

Gold and silver is still the Constitutional money of the United States, and guns are still specifically protected.

So long as the Constitution is recognized as the Supreme Law of the Land, although presently disregarded, its shield of individual sovereignty, presents an impenetrable barrier to world control advocates.

'PRESIDENT BUSH'S, "COTTON PICKING" EDUCATION!
"Horse Sense, Is Stable Thinking"
(Burl Daniel, my now departed father in law.)* my opinion.
***From Either End Of The Horse!**

This old working boy from Lubbock, doesn't possess the Ivy League degree possessed by the man from Midland. And rather than flying airplanes in the Texas National Guard, I dug 81mm mortar emplacements, in the twenty degree below zero weather of Grafenvere Germany. ***10th Infantry-86th Regiment-1955-56.***

However, many working people consider a degree in Innate Common Sense; obtained from the University of Hard Knocks; although Politically Incorrect; of more value.

Nothing could better establish this as fact, Mr. President, than your current position, that there are many jobs Americans simply won't do, therefore, we must import Mexican laborers by the millions, while forgiving the mis-conduct of millions more, whose very presence, constitutes criminal trespass.

Obviously oil patch economics, don't square with cotton patch economics, and apparently the laws of supply and demand aren't taught at Yale, and certainly not from the perspective of an old "bole puller," ***therefore, I will attempt to augment your Ivy League Degree, with a "cotton picking education," from my Vocational Ag point of view.***

For the purpose of explanation, let's assume that at one time, a valuable resource was discovered in a kingdom we will call Texas, the resource we will call oil. A great demand soon developed for this resource, with Texas a prime producer.

Very shortly, an organization, we will call the Seven Sisters, a consortium of producers, persuaded a government entity, we will call the Texas Railroad Commission too assume the task of setting and maintaining the price.

This feat was accomplished by limiting the amount of oil

produced by each well over a given period of time, while bestowing upon the producers, a 27% federal tax break, in the form of a "depletion allowance."

Are you with me so far Mr. President?

The possible profit, as well as the tax break, made exploration, though expensive, very appealing too a lot of people, thus, prospective land was leased all over the Kingdom of Texas; "doodle bug" drilling rigs, and seismograph crews could not be assembled fast enough.

The demand, thus, the profit was so great, that the Seven Sisters were soon searching for profitable sources, all over the world. They were successful in a Kingdom we will call Arabia.

The rulers of the kingdom, possessing not a clue as too the true worth of the oil, signed contracts with the Seven Sisters, awarding them control of the oil, for a price bordering on theft.

Rather than being required to drill wells thousands of feet deep, and then pump the oil out of the ground, as was the case in the Kingdom of Texas, in the Kingdom of Arabia, the process required hardly more than punching a hole in the ground a few feet deep, and then collecting the oil as it flowed to the surface.

Thus, the oil could be imported and sold, for a price that rendered exploration in The Kingdom of Texas unprofitable, ultimately, many under financed, former producers, "wild catters," and "doodle buggers," stacked their drilling rigs, some after going broke.

In a nut shell, this is the reality of supply and demand.

Guess what Mr. President; this same system works equally well with cotton production, milk production, beef production, or even labor.

Apparently you have never been affected by unfair foreign

competition; are a very slow study; or just don't care, whether or not common citizens earn a wage sufficient too adequately care for our families, *so long as your corporate gravy train, glides on rails of dirt cheap labor.*

The essence of the lesson is: *The importation of cheap labor, by increasing the available supply, will drive the value of domestic labor down to imported level, a level which will continue to fall, in direct proportion to the total importation, eventually Equalizing, At The Third World Level!*

Once again the law and currency manipulators get the gold, and, as usual, we, the unrepresented, get the shaft!

Contrarily, without artificial competition, the value of domestic labor will rise, resulting in the equalization of the negotiating position of management and labor; "Presto" a wage attractive enough too entice those in the domestic workforce, to accept jobs formerly refused; Especially if We Quit Paying Them Not to Work.

Our Next "Cotton Picking" Lesson Is On The Use Of Wealth!

Although Our Nation is Now Drowning in Red Ink, our *Non-Representatives* to the Federal Government, continue to throw escalating quantities of wealth, *yet to be created*, by *citizens yet to be born*, at problems created by their own incompetent mis-handling of existing wealth, created by the present, as well as past generations.

Although government is up to its ears in bankruptcy; while over its head, and out of its element in domestic, as well as business affairs, we are assured by our current Federal Government officials that: "we will "grow" our way out of this mess!"

Sure We Will El Presidente!

Just as the merchant losing money on every sale, will recoup his money with high sales volume, mortgaged assets, and

concealed/denied, business expenses!

While The Cost of Education Skyrockets, with your blessing, aid, and complicity of our elected *Non-Representatives*; through the importation of competition, and exporting of opportunity, its value is plummeting; as is the value of domestic skilled, educated, and experienced labor.

The Situation Then Gets Even More Bazaar, And Insulting, as you, and the rest of "*our Non-Representative government,*" are now promoting a plan; *Implemented With Tax Revenue,* which, with welfare, "amnesty," education, medical care, and social security benefits; augment the value of cheaper, illegal labor, thereby totally destroying the value, of legal, domestic labor!

Translation: We, The Lawful Citizenry, Must Purchase The Knife, With Which Our Throats Are Being Cut!

Adding Injure To The Insults: With encouragement from your buddy, President Vicente Fox of Mexico, illegal immigrants, severely lacking knowledge of our laws; can neither read, nor understand the language; possess little driving experience in our traffic; even now, are being issued drivers license, and "identity cards," *With Which They May Not Only Operate Huge Trucks On Our Roads, But Register To Vote, In Our National Elections!*

Has our "leadership" become so saturated, thus corrupted, with New World Order Globalism, that we, a nation of sovereign individuals, who could not be taken by armies, is simply being betrayed into subjugation, by that "leadership?"

If This Is So, The American People Would Be Far Better Served By Anarchy!

Come on Mr. Bush, although many of your fellow Americans, by your standards, and apparently those of our elected *Non-Representatives*, may be uneducated, we are not stupid! (at least some of us)

With the cost of "financing" our government, your war, and the just detailed policies destroying the value of our time; endangering our lives and welfare; eating up our children's future; and allowing anyone in the world a say in the selection of our "leadership," many of us are in need of being enlightened, as to the current advantages of American citizenship.

Our Next "Cotton Picking" Lesson, Is On Domestic Security! You Know, Protecting Our Own Nest And Livelihood!

Because your recently proposed program, in essence, amounts to a pipeline, through which prodigious quantities of currency flows into Mexico, thereby simplifying his job, it is very easy to understand President Fox's enthusiasm.

Mexico possesses the potential of being one of the richest nations on earth. It enjoys one of the most favorable climates on the globe.

Spectacular salt water beaches, and abundant sunshine translates into a bottomless treasure chest, into which tourist pour an endless supply of wealth.

Gold and silver was so plentiful, and so easily attained, that they possessed no special value to the ancient inhabitants.

However, once discovered by Spanish explorers, their value unleashed a torrent of cruelty, barbarism, and heartache, typified by Montezuma's kidnapping and imprisonment, and, because his ransom was not assembled quickly enough to suit the Spanish government, his execution.

To this day, we are salvaging sunken remnants of their "plate fleet," assembled for the sole purpose of transporting soldiers and priest too, and looted wealth from, the "land of endless treasure."

The priest for the purpose of convincing the natives of the

"righteousness" of obeying their new slave masters, and the soldiers for the purpose of "encouraging" those who resisted the priestly overtures.

This first encounter with "civilized government," unfortunately became the pattern of "leadership" which has plagued the nation for hundreds of years.

Even now, there is no reason, other than mis-management of secular leadership, and over population, thanks to encouragement from the religious, for Mexico's financial hardship!

When coupled with the tourist magnet, she has enough tillable, as well as range land, in addition to natural resources, including silver and oil, to easily care for the entire population in grand style.

President Fox should consider it a personal failure, that Mexican citizens must leave their families, and work for slave labor wages in another land, under his watch.

It is no secret to those of us raised in, and thus familiar with the Southwestern part of the United States, and this of course includes you, Mr. President, that the "government" of Mexico, has, for hundreds of years, amounted to nothing more than the personification of greed, corruption, and institutionalized crime.

The Federalle roams the countryside, constantly harassing the various bandit gangs, not for the purpose of protecting the citizenry, but too stamp out any budding revolt, or, because the government does not appreciate the competition.

International law, has for thousands of years, and in every case, supported the right of any nation to control access to their sovereign territory. Thus, the propensity too disregard recognized borders, has, for millennia, been considered a very serious offense, with lethal enforcement procedures, both permitted and embraced, at the desecration of the aggrieved nation.

Boundary disputes, as evidenced by history, provide the impetus for very nearly every war; how then can anyone dispute the fact, that *the purpose of government, Above All Else, is the security of "the nest;" the very foundation of the stable family, as well as both personal, and common wealth?*

Even the American Eagle Recognizes This Fact!

While we could find the funds to defend the borders of Kuwait, an army of millions of people, bearing millions of tons of poison to be distributed to our children, have, over at least the last fifty years, poured virtually unchecked into our nation.

This conduit, extending from the tip of South America, to the northern border of Mexico, is certainly no secret to the residents of California, Arizona, New Mexico and Texas, Nor The Federal Politicians!

That any state must even request aid, for the defense of national borders, indicts our Non-Representatives, on the charge of dereliction of the duty to protect their fellow citizens welfare from foreign threats: the basic responsibility, to which they were elected!

While one billion dollars per week can be poured into Iraq for the purpose of "nation building," *sufficient resources and personnel have never been allocated too the protection of our own borders.*

Mr. President, if these resources and resolve were dedicated to our own security, there would be little need to antagonize the citizens of foreign lands with our presence. *Given the current state of technology, within a few short months, a fly couldn't get into this nation without being detected!*

Yet not one of our Presidents, past or present, nor any of our Non-Representatives, until now, just prior to our current elections,

have displayed any desire to fulfill this most basic of duties. Instead, <u>many of them have directed their efforts, toward the disarming of We The People!</u>

Contrarily, the "leadership" of the United States, is now in open discussion with the current "leadership" of Mexico,(a nation which has for decades, encouraged total disregard for our immigration laws) <u>not for the purpose of curtailing the criminal conduct, but, in a conspiracy to reward it!</u>

Mr. Bush, you as President, and everyone of our other Non-Representatives, took an oath too protect and defend our Constitution and obey its laws, as the price of the key to the office too which you, and they, had been elected: Yet--------

<u>And Let's Get This Straight!</u>

While we the people, are watching our civil rights disappear in the name of national" security:

Endure "swat" team raids in our living rooms, for the purpose of verifying *suspicions;* of the *suspected* presence; of the *possiblity* of drugs; *Drugs Which, If Present, Should Have Been Interdicted At Our Borders* ; though, if confirmed, *will justify any and all deaths occurring in the confiscation process:*

Weave our way around armed soldiers at our airports:

Greet our youth as they arrive home in body bags:

Pour a billion dollars per week down the money pit of Iraq, and hundreds of lives of our youth, attempting too aid and control their people:

Annually provide billions of dollars, and an army of our youth, needlessly protecting the security of nations around the globe:

Send more "foreign aid" than we can count too Israel, so they can steal more Arab land, build a wall around it, and kill anyone

with the audacity to protest:

You appear on world wide TV, singing praise; extolling virtues; proposing amnesty and citizenship; while offering the Presidential hand to millions of criminals, you anticipate addressing as "My Fellow Americans."

Mr. President, We Do Not Owe, Nor Should We Provide, An Overflow For Mexico's Surplus Population!

A Compendium Of Facts, Anyone Of Which Is Alarming, But When Combined, Comprise A Damning Commentary On Our "Damn-ocratic" Government!

Perhaps this makes sense to the man from Midland, his Ivy League Alumni, and our *Non-Representatives*, but, to an old, uneducated working man from Lubbock: It Stinks Too High Heaven!

How about we, the current citizenry, either unemployed, or underemployed, as the result of government policies which have exported our employment opportunities to foreign shores?

Will laws against stealing, shoplifting, burglary, robbery and car theft, be overlooked, when committed by good, God fearing individuals, for the purpose of feeding their families, or the acquisition of dependable transportation?

As far as the excuse that Americans will not do the jobs--although I have visited Midland a few times, I never realized that in the hundred or so miles between the Lubbock cotton patch, and the Midland oil patch, that economics could get so screwed up, nor, why it should be so hard to understand that: When you quit paying people not too work, you observe an immediate change in attitude!"

Exemplified by the conversation between two old Idaho farmers, in which one was complaining about the high cost of feeding his dogs.

"I just feed my dogs good Idaho potatoes, right out of the field" responded his friend.

"But my dogs won't eat potatoes, exclaimed the first!"

Too which his friend again responded, "Neither would mine, for about two weeks."

Our Next "Cotton Picking" Lesson, Is In Getting Your Ducks In A Row!

Mr. President, it is apparent that even in Midland, you spent very few, if any, twelve hour shifts freezing your ass off working evening tower,(top platform on a drilling derrick) and have, in all likelihood, never laid eyes on a cotton sack.

While I never worked evening tower, although I have friends, who, on their journey up the ladder to "tool pusher"(crew boss) have; in my teen years, I spent many hours on my knees filling sixteen to twenty foot cotton sacks; oh, did I forget to mention that this was also true of my younger brother and sister, although with shorter sacks.

I know that perhaps it now seems a little strange, but in the nineteen forties, many parents were of the opinion that children should be taught to work. Our parents held strong beliefs along these lines, as did Mr. and Mrs. Ray, not only close neighbors, and farmers, but parents of our closest friends, school chums, and playmates.

I don't know what Betty, Lilly, and Vanita had their eyes on, but the Dennis kids were all focused on new bicycles, and mom was prepared to help us acquire them.

Mr. Ray set aside a field for us to harvest; so after school and on Saturdays, the three Dennis kids, and the three Ray girls, with mom coordinating the tasks, keeping weights, and pulling boles; in the late fall, with our money, and her contributions, our

dreams became reality!

If you are hungry, (thanks to my father I never was) or, have your eye on a new bicycle, or perhaps some high school "wheels," work not only doesn't look so bad; and, I think the Ray girls will concur; *our stint in the cotton patch, was a very enjoyable experience.*

Good friends, good neighbors, good parents, and less intrusive government, is a winning combination.

Speaking of government, the legal importation of cheap labor, amounts too nothing more than dis-honestly sneaking, what is legitimately referred too as wage and price controls, in through the back door!

Neither the welfare of the Mexican work force, *nor the acquisition of cheap domestic labor,* is the responsibility of any member of our elected government, especially the President!

According to the Declaration of Independence, the power of government is derived from the consent of the governed, thus, our government, by relieving the economic distress, simultaneously preserves tolerance of the status quo, forestalling the day that the Mexican citizenry demand proper government; a day long overdue, but so far unsought.

Contrarily; the United States, thanks to our forefathers, was, after fighting for the opportunity, built, maintained and defended, with blood, sweat, tears, and unbelievable hardship; and its purpose re-defined, by yet another war.

Reward criminal conduct, by cheapening the value of American citizenship?

Like Hell!

Send them home, and let them devote their labor and talents, toward the development of their own nations potential!

I know from first hand experience that there are many jobs in this nation that are not pleasant, and some downright revolting. However, some member or members of our citizenry, have, on every occasion, stepped forward and begun clawing their way through the mountain of horse dung, in search of the horse, as the nation itself attests.

All achieved by native born individuals? Certainly Not!

But, with the contributions of immigrants who played by the rules; respected the laws of what they hoped would be their new home; awaited due process; and then with pride, worked by day, and studied by night, toward the day when they could proudly declare themselves, American Citizens!

Even The Thought Of Rewarding Unlawful Entry With Amnesty, Pardon or Citizenship, Dishonors Every Citizen Who Respects Our Heritage, By Obeying Our Nations Laws!

Our Next "Cotton Picking" Lesson, Obesity, Government Style!

While personal obesity is now being recognized as a threat to the health of the citizenry, government obesity and gluttony, is destroying the nations health, wealth, and welfare; The Very Freedoms Upon Which It Feeds.

Yet, while our *Non-Representatives* are eager to assist in "solving" the individuals problem, (not their responsibility) not one of them is considering solving the nations out of control spending and debt problem.(most certainly their responsibility)

A hint: The best thing you, our *Non-Representatives* can do, after first shifting the tax advantage away from multi-national corporations, and back to Individual Businesses, is take a long vacation, and reflect upon the following: *The US doesn't need an influx of foreign workers: We Need Fewer, Far Fewer Politicians, and Less, Much Less Government.*

Contrary to the propaganda, governments do not create wealth

producing jobs!

Governments impose obstruction to, and demands upon, individuals attempting to create new job opportunities, while claiming first rights to a portion of any wealth which any new job manages to create.

It is absolutely insulting, that the work force of the nation, should be required to defend what money we do manage to acquire, from government thieves in the guise of tax collectors, and to be threatened with prison for failure to "properly" account for it.

Our Next "Cotton Picking" Lesson, Is On The Ordering Of Priorities."

The motivation to become a *Non-Representative*, is, to a great extent the desire to fulfill a personal vision of just what the nation could become, if only it were structured according to their philosophy, with its wealth dedicated to the achievement of their goals.

If only the United States were dedicated to the service of God, as an example, there would be no more hunger, pain, and suffering-- our thoughts would all be pure, and we would live in a violence free environment.

Nice thought, in fact the thought which has, since the beginning of recorded history, been the foundation of one bloody, dictatorial, maniacal government, right after another, to this very day.

Think not! Then re-read the Old Testament of the Christian Bible, and examine: Roman Catholic, Spanish Catholic, and Islamic history, from its inception.

Even in the United States, a religiously inspired Constitutional Amendment, number Eighteen to be exact, was enacted, which, for the first time denied, rather than protected, the right of

individual self determination.

By the time of its repeal by the Twenty-first, the Federal Government had been empowered, and did in fact, create agencies with the "right" to act, without consequence, outside the law.

Supposedly a declaration of war on alcohol, it was instead a war on common sense, the criminal justice system in general, and the civil rights of every American in particular.

As justice was taken out of the courts, and deposited with "law enforcement," the nation became a prison, and several of our major cities, major war zones.

Shorn of their right to exist by the Twenty-first, the agencies created by the implementing authority of the Eighteenth, should have died with it!

However, as is very vividly revealed by the general "war on drugs," and the war on specific American citizenry, as typified at Ruby Ridge Idaho, and Waco Texas, such was not the case!

We The People must realize, and act upon the knowledge, that excessive resources and "rights," when deposited with law enforcement, does not achieve a risk free, work free, society, contrarily, it is the kiss of death to any civilization.

Because it stifles creativity, inhibits dreams, and denies the opportunity to achieve the much needed sense of growth and personal fulfillment, a government working toward these goals, while educating the citizenry to accept such a concept, is not only weakening its moral foundation, but is destroying the economic foundation of the nation.

Talk About Some Screwed Up Priorities!

The "mortgage our nations future" governmental policy, so extremely damaging to the American family, is revealed by incarceration figures, drug addiction, and rampant school age sex, etc.

Our current, as well as following generations, extending into the forever, are imprisoned in a straightjacket of debt, thus, both parents are forced out of the home, and away from children during the most critical, developmental period of their lives.

Why then, Mr. President, rather than devoting your efforts toward the elimination of the freedom devouring national debt; *a true crisis;* are you, and many of our *Non-Representatives,* focusing your efforts toward amending the Constitution for "The Defense of Marriage?"

Marriage Needs No Defense!

We The People are quite capable of determining for ourselves, just what it is, and what it isn't, without another Constitutional amendment, again denying, rather than defending, individual rights.

What We Do Need, is a Constitutional Amendment in the Defense of Our Nation, From Irresponsible Politicians, By The Mandating Of A Balanced Budget!

The interchangeable terms Damn-ocracy / Dam-ocracy---Damn-ocratic / Dam-ocratic and Damn-ocrat / Dam-ocrat--when used in this book, as terms best supportive of my contentions, are defined as follows:

Any form of government, encompassing *Any economic system,* staffed by *Any individual,* too which, or to whom, the descriptions or contentions, are appropriate!

Read the book, and then ask yourself why any of the current government should be re-elected!

THE VALUE OF TIME

TIME: a seemingly innocuous word, for the most valuable of assets! Let's qualify that statement, TIME: The most valuable asset of the human race.

Time is Life! ~~ Time is Money!

Repeat After Me and Act Accordingly!

Time Is Personal Property, at its Basic Level!

WHAT IS YOUR TIME WORTH?

How are you presently utilizing, what should be your most prized possession?

Do you agree with "professional managements" policy, of introducing currency into the "economy" by overfilling the law and currency manipulators feed (hog) trough, and allowing we "turkey's," that which "trickles" down?

If not, get mad, get registered to vote, and get rid of "Dam-ocracy," by electing people who understand the value of true Republican government, and will guarantee to govern accordingly!

Every human being upon drawing his/her first breath, simultaneously acquires a finite allotment of time; our journey of mortal life has begun; a journey preordained too inevitably terminate as a date with death.

Time is linear, it can be neither stopped nor started, and not one second will ever be reclaimed, once gone-gone for good!

How the time, relentlessly streaming from our lives is used, or "spent, is governed, to a great extent, by the conditions created

as the result of its use, by the many individuals preceding us in this common journey, down the path of mortal life.

Although we have no control over its flow; can neither conserve nor recover even one second; we were blessed with the resources to enhance its value, <u>beginning with our awesome brain.</u>

Our closest approach to a time bank, is in the accumulation of artifacts and knowledge.

Every time we turn on a light, get into our car, or even take a cookie from the cookie jar, we are reaping the accumulative rewards of the productive use of time, extending all the way back to the discovery of the first, of the many uses for fire.

The will to live--self preservation, is the most prevalent of impulses, whether the entity is the smallest micro-organism, or the largest whale, however, only the human species is time oriented.

A honey bee is one of the most productive, goal oriented, protective entities on earth. Although preceding the human species by eons of time, their evolution of knowledge, thus technology, is non-existent, consequently, nothing is of less value to either the individual bee, or the collective, than a time piece.

The same is true of the chimpanzee, our closest relative in the animal kingdom, and yes, unfortunately it is even true of many of our fellow human beings.

From the beginning of human kinds tenure on the planet, traded for food, clothing and shelter, time has served the role of money, yet its true value is seldom considered, and even more rarely appreciated.

The right of determining the value of time, as well as its use, is retained only by people living in nations with governments that

acknowledge, and govern, in accordance with the fact, that Time Is Indeed, Personal Property, At Its Basic Level !

In the beginning, the securing of the necessities of life, consumed virtually every waking hour; even today, in some parts of the world, these necessities are impossible to attain in either adequate quantity or quality, regardless of the amount of time dedicated to the effort.

Under these circumstances, when futility and utter hopelessness become constant companions, and destitution the reality of the past, present and foreseeable future, TIME not only possess minimal value, but vanishes, both unnoticed, and unmourned, the ultimate tragedy!

Thankfully these circumstances were not the norm, and the indomitable human spirit would not be denied the opportunity, to not only survive, but prosper.

Without question, our ancestors became aware early on, that by voluntarily contributing their various aptitudes to a common effort, each participant could enjoy a better standard of living, with less effort and aggravation.

While cooperation facilitated the task, obtaining the basic necessities still dominated virtually every thought, and consumed virtually every minute, of every day.

The value of TIME was not appreciated, until it could be traded for things other than the bare essentials of life.

In all likelihood, the first beneficiaries of "FREE TIME" were men possessing either the craftiness or might, to persuade or compel others, to devote their time, to his welfare.

Artifacts and records of ancient Egypt, offer very intriguing testimony to this statement, as well as to their appreciation of the value derived from the dedication of each individuals unique aptitudes toward a common goal.

VALUE OF TIME

From very early history, advanced cultures have existed in which the time of the ordinary citizen was both recognized and prized.

Invariably however, their prosperity, both envied and coveted, were overwhelmed by barbarians from without, or treachery from within.

Their riches plundered, squandered, and citizens enslaved, the world would enter another "dark age."

The world was in the initial stages of emergence from one of these periodic plights, just prior to the birth of the United States.

Our nations founders, very familiar with various forms of government, considered several, including democracy and monarchy, before choosing the republican form.

In a Monarchy, the "subjects" time belongs to the King/Queen, in a Totalitarian regime, the "dictator," and under Communism, the collective, administered by elitist committee.

Democracy,(mob rule) because it offers the illusion of individual sovereignty, and the allure of something for nothing, is the most deceiving.

It creates a natural association of those individuals with no desire to work, and those with the desire to achieve personal philosophical goals, using other people's money.

A constituency constructed of a composite of many interacting groups, by simple majority vote, create laws appropriating the wealth of the productive segment of society, and, by employing the power of government to enforce those laws, destroy individual sovereignty, even their own.

Government representatives, elected by majority vote, assume control of the public treasury then use the power of "public" money to maintain their positions in authority. A very insidious arrangement.

Very cognizant of these facts, and very leery of centralized power, our nations founders attempted to thwart the possibilities of domestic chicanery with the founding documents.

Had their efforts been successful, this book would not be needful.

While we have very successfully fought off the enemy from without, just as feared, civil authority granted, has been utilized to acquire power denied, freedom devouring power--expanding exponentially.

Less than two hundred years ago, death and misery, as the result of disease and famine, was prevalent in much of the world, and even today, hopelessness is still the reality faced by many people.

As previously noted, the enormous potential and purpose to which the human race was created, is impossible to achieve without cooperation and the segmenting of each task.

The implementation and perfecting of this principle, became the very foundation of the United States.

With the evidence of its success so prominently displayed, and so widely acknowledged, the following question is inevitable.

Why would anyone now benefiting from the enviable success of a system based upon individual freedom and initiative, and the envy of the world, work toward its destruction, or, at least its alteration? The Answer:

From day one, coexisting with the industrious segment of society, individuals who are willing to exchange their time for their living, are those, with a passion to direct, and the desire to live well off the efforts of their fellow human beings, the human parasites!

This theme is prevalent throughout this book, so, to set the record straight, *I Do Not Hate Management!* Management is a division of labor, and is absolutely essential, to the productive use of time!

Good management however, because their personal welfare, as well as pride, is tied directly to the profitability of an enterprise, manage with not only these factors in mind, but, with dedication to excellence in any endeavor in which they are involved, as do other craftsmen.

They do not "manage" a company into bankruptcy, and then draw a multi-million dollar "bonus" for doing so!

These people are not managers, they are law, currency, and people manipulators, and exploiters.

With greed the motivating factor, rather than pride in a job well done, any company, or, enterprise, with which they are involved, is in deep trouble from the beginning!

The "pooling" of labor, and its compounding effect on the value of time, is the building block of human civilization, and the only means by which our awesome potential may be realized.

Not one of us is granted the specialized intelligence to understand the entire complexity of our reality, nor the physical capabilities to perform anything more than a bare minimum of the tasks basic to our individual survival.

The requirement of physical labor can no more be separated from the reality of human existence, than can either of the sexes, both are part and parcel of mortal life.

These concepts are so obvious too me, that the contempt of many, and even absolute abhorrence of others, of those individuals supplying the physical labor required in the actual

construction and maintenance of their places of residence, is mystifying.

Perhaps it is difficult for some people to understand, but fifty years ago, the majority of Americans not only did not abhor, but enjoyed physical labor!

Many of us still do!

Although testimony to our education is the physical reality of the nation itself, the absence of diplomas accrediting that education, categorizes us, not as crucial components, the absence of which relegates the efforts of planners and managers too nothing more than exercises in futility, but as virtually worthless idiots, too stupid too escape manual labor.

Thus, we have become a nation of managers, merchandisers, sales clerks, and law and currency manipulators, however, *we are managing, merchandising, and selling that produced by foreign "idiots," with no aversion to manual labor, as once was true of the United States.*

The national debt and balance of payment deficit is not the fault of the American work force!

The people of this nation, comprise the most industrious work force the world has every seen. We are workaholic's! World wide, no other nations even comes close too the per capita time devoted to work.

There is absolutely no reason, other than government mis-management, and fraud, for this nation to be in debt.

In The Name of Capitalism:

Our "Professional Management," has, with the aid of Rothschilds "Bogus Dollars," and a "fiscal policy" instituted for the purpose of "fighting inflation," by *intentionally reducing the value of our labor:*

"Managed" too rob the last two generations of the American family, of much of the motherly influence necessary to the correct development of our children:

Divested our nation of the worlds best production system:

Flushed one of the best work forces to ever exist down the toilet:

Sold our following generations into slavery:

Totally destroyed a positive balance of payment accounts ledger:

All in a time span of forty years!

While the concern over impending inflation gets the blame, in reality, inflation in this instance may be summed up thusly:

The reflection of the accumulative cost of government; combined with practices and policies which have decreased the efficiency of labor, production, and transportation; thereby diminishing the volume, as well as merchantability of the nations exportable product.

In a nutshell, our nations productively has been in chains for the last fifty years, as reflected by our national debt, and balance of trade deficit.

Our contribution too the scheme of things, has been fifty years of relative peace, maintained by constantly developing military technology, thus weapons strength; *coupled with the grossly under paid services integrity, and competence of our youth, as well as our military leadership.*

We have been in the past, and are currently, living off the efforts of a few million of our nations finest citizenry, *while confiscating their future, with unpayable debt.*

VALUE OF TIME

This corrupt finance/government system, has robbed the nation of far more than its productivity, and, previously positive, balance of payments ledger.

Optimism, the former characterizing trait of the nation, has been replaced with anxiety, futility, boredom, and constant frustration, as fruitful work disappears.

The prevailing atmosphere is that of a coiled spring, compressed ever tighter, as the result of the desperate efforts to either justify, or, obscure, the consumption of vast wealth, as well as freedoms, now disappearing at a prodigious rate.

With a tax system that penalizes success and hard work, many of our citizens are now convinced, that their only hope of financial prosperity is through gambling, thus desperation is now driving many people too divert ever increasing quantities of their income, into this "investment."

How has the nation been so transformed, in so short a period of time? The answer!

Trust Disarms Vigilance!

The current situation is the result of: the natural progression of an unstable system; creating a constant stream of disenchanted citizens; professionally manipulated by individuals acting upon their ambition to dictate the course of world affairs!

What type of government could possibly be better devised to create, merge and dominate, a growing army of distraught people, than a "Damnocracy?"

With the passage of time, the increasing complexity inherent in the division of labor, while creating a greater dependence upon the collective, has greatly minimized the importance of the individual, thus diminishing the appreciation of their role in the overall scheme of things.

While encompassing ever increasing numbers of individuals, each contributing to the final outcome, like concentric waves in a pool of water, those individuals comprising the rings furthest from the epicenter, tend too lose sight of, or, were never aware of the final goal.

Thus, as their contributions go unrecognized, and their wages decrease, they are both dismayed, and disillusioned.

While this may pose few problems in a society based upon the ascendancy of the collective at the expense of the individual, it represents a huge problem, for a nation which at least propagandizes, the importance of the individual.

The strength of the fledgling United States was cooperation, neighbor helping neighbor, in good times and bad. Men and women, who, in the space of one hundred years, with native intelligence and hard work, transformed a nation still oozing the blood of brothers from its soil, into a tribute to human resourcefulness.

This feat was accomplished while defending our right to exist, fielding an army and furnishing the equipment to defeat two massive military machines, and providing the wealth and ingenuity too rebuild much of the world, *Without Acquiring Massive Debt.*

Following World War II, their duty completed, many men stepped off the battle field onto collage campuses, assisted financially by state and federal governments, and their wives.

Having proven their aptitude and worth in the work force, many women enthusiastically relinquished their jobs too the returning men, others did so quite reluctantly.

Unlike today, a very large percentage of the acquired knowledge, was in fields augmenting productive manual labor; the cultivation of productive work skills, not those of avoidance.

Powered by manual labor, applied ingenuity and technological advances, real wealth production, and the standard of living went off the scale, while happiness and optimism, vanquished hopelessness and futility, not only in this nation, but in much of the world.

Diagnosing the factors driving our current economic plight is, as expressed in the vernacular of the day, "A Slam Dunk!"

Without Question:

Socialist Damn-ocracy, beginning with the federal reserve, must be dismantled and replaced with a self governing Republic, the government of the Declaration of Independence.

Constitutional money, as guaranteed each state, must be restored!

Our current legal system must be junked, and replaced with Constitutional practices and Constitutional law, written in common English, as taught in K thru 12th grade.

States rights, responsibilities, and resources, per the Constitution, must be restored!

Only Then Can We: THROW THE THIEVES OUT OF THE TIME VAULT!

THE COMMANDEERED DOLLAR

United States Congressional Record - March 17, 1993 - Vol. #33, page H-1303 -
Speaker~Rep. James Traficant, Jr. (Ohio) has been yielded the floor for a period of four minutes for the purpose of addressing the House of Representatives, he begins: "Mr. Speaker, we are here now in chapter 11. Members of Congress are official trustees presiding over the greatest reorganization of any bankrupt entity in world history, the US Government. We are setting forth hopefully, a blueprint for our future. There are some who say it is a coroner's report that will lead to our demise........

United States Bankruptcy! How The Hell Did That Happen?

The bankruptcy referred to is merely one of the periodically recurring symptoms of the bankruptcy of 1933, at which time Franklin Roosevelt, and the Democratic Congress, robbed the nations citizenry of its lawful money.

The 1971 episode in which Richard Nixon closed the gold window to foreign nations, thereby forcing the world economic system to embrace a fiat currency, or lose the largest market for their manufactured products, was another symptom.

Many Americans were not old enough in the 1970's to remember the depression of the 1930's, and those that had lived through the era, did not associate it with bankruptcy.

Although many of us remember the effects, we did not, and still do not, relate it to bankruptcy. In fact, the vast majority of us have never considered the concept of government bankruptcy, especially the bankruptcy of the American government, so a brief recap:

In the early to mid 1970's, the United States found itself in crisis; the story, very heavily publicized through out the United States,

was that there was a very severe shortage of oil.

It was very strange to most of us, that although we had been engaged in war for years, and all the while awash in oil, that with the war ending, suddenly there was a shortage.

However, after having been "properly educated "for a few weeks, by some aggravating waits in gas lines and restrictions on quantity, and after having grudgingly accepted some serious price increases, "Presto," instantaneously oil was again as plentiful as water.

It was later revealed, that throughout the entire crisis, tankers, loaded to overflowing, were lined up just off shore. The crisis it turned out, had been manufactured by the United States government, in order to justify some very necessary price increases for domestic oil, and to justify inflation triggered by fighting a war on credit--the inflation which was reducing the value of the dollars foreign suppliers received in exchange for their oil.

Reportedly, as the result of some serious negotiations, the troublesome Arab nations had agreed to invest rather heavily in the latest military equipment and training--20 year annuities, with the yield tied to the rate of inflation--and gold. It was however, the opinion of many experts, that the entire episode had been engineered by the Banking Syndicate.

How did the United States get into financial difficulty, with so much tax money coming in?

The short answer: *FEDERAL RESERVE.*

The Fed Act of 1913, from its inception, was not popular legislation! The Democratic party assailed it, and in the election campaign of 1912, many ran upon the rejection of the idea of transferring the duties assigned to Congress by the Constitution, to a private banking system. In fact, many considered it too be

totally unconstitutional.

However, on December 23, 1913, taking advantage of the Christmas break, thus the absence of Legislators opposed to its creation, the Federal Reserve Act was passed.

In 1934, during the great depression, Congressman Louis T. McFadden, a long time Chairman of the Committee on Banking and Currency, asked for criminal conspiracy investigations by Congress, thereby setting the stage for a planned abolishment of the privately owned Federal Reserve System, and prosecution of those responsible, where possible.

He requested impeachment of Federal officials who had violated oaths of office, both in establishing and directing the Federal Reserve, beseeching Congress to investigate overt criminal acts by the Federal Reserve Board, and Federal Reserve Banks.

The McFadden speech clearly suggested the possibility that the Federal Reserve deliberately triggered the great stock market crash of 1929, for the purpose of promoting the passage of the Emergency Banking Act of March 9, 1933, the act which suspended the gold standard.

A portion of the speech follows. For your enlightenment I strongly urge you to devote the time to read at least that part. The speech, in its entirety is to be published on the "Damocracy.net" web site.

As recorded within the Congressional Record, beginning with House pages 1295... Quote:
Mr. Chairman we have in this Country one of the most corrupt institutions the world has ever known. I refer to the Federal Reserve Board and the Federal Reserve Banks, hereinafter called the Fed.

The Fed has cheated the Government of these United States, and the people of the United States, out of enough money to pay the Nation's debt. The depredations and iniquities of the Fed has

cost this Country enough money to pay the National debt several times over.

This evil institution has impoverished and ruined the people of these United States, has bankrupted itself, and has practically bankrupted our Government. (emphasis added)
It has done this through the defects of law under which it operates, through the mis-administration of that law, and through the corrupt practices of the moneyed vultures who control it.

Some people think that the Federal Reserve Banks are United States Government institutions. They are private monopolies which prey upon the people of these United States for the benefit of themselves and their foreign customers, foreign and domestic speculators and swindlers, and rich, predatory money lenders.

In that dark crew of financial pirates, there are those who would cut a man's throat to get a dollar out of his pocket; there are those who send money into states to buy votes to control our legislatures; there are those who maintain international propaganda for the purpose of deceiving us into granting of new concessions which will permit them to cover up their past misdeeds, and set again in motion, their gigantic train of crime.

These twelve private credit monopolies were deceitfully and disloyally foisted upon this Country by the bankers who came here from Europe, and repaid us our hospitality by undermining our American institutions.

Those bankers took money out of this Country to finance Japan in a war against Russia.

They created a reign of terror in Russia, with our money, in order to help that war along.

They instigated the separate peace between Germany and Russia, and thus drove a wedge between the Allies in the World War.

They financed Trotsky's passage from New York to Russia, so that he might assist in the destruction of the Russian Empire.

They fomented and instigated the Russian Revolution, and placed a large fund of American dollars at Trotsky's disposal in one of their branch banks in Sweden, that through him, Russian homes might be thoroughly broken up, and Russian children flung far and wide from their natural protectors.

They have since begun breaking up American homes, and the dispersal of American children.

Mr. Chairman, there should be no partisanship in matters concerning banking and currency affairs in this Country, and I do not speak with any.

In 1912, the National Monetary Association, under the chairmanship of the late Senator Nelson W. Aldrich, made a report, and presented a vicious bill, called the National Reserve Association bill. This bill is usually spoken of as the Aldrich bill. Senator Aldrich did not write the Aldrich bill. He was the tool, if not the accomplice, of the European bankers who for nearly twenty years had been scheming to set up a central bank in this Country, and, who in 1912, had spent, and were continuing to spend, vast sums of money to accomplish their purpose. We were opposed to the Aldrich plan for a central bank.

The men who rule the Democratic Party, then promised the people that if they were returned to power ,there would be no central bank established here while they held the reigns of government. (emphasis added) Thirteen months later that promise was broken, and the Wilson administration, under the tutelage of those sinister Wall Street figures who stood behind Colonel House, established here, in our free Country, the worm-eaten, monarchical institution, of the "King's Bank," to control us from the top downward, and to shackle us from the cradle to the grave.

The Federal Reserve Bank destroyed our old and characteristic way of doing business. It discriminated against our 1-name commercial paper, the finest in the world, and it set up the antiquated 2-name paper, which is the present curse of this Country, and has wrecked every country to which it was given scope. It fastened down upon the Country, the very tyranny from which the framers of the Constitution sought to save us.

One of the greatest battles for the preservation of this Republic was fought out here in Jackson's time, when the second Bank of the United States, founded on the same false principles of those which are here exemplified in the Fed, was hurled out of existence.

After that, in 1837, the Country was warned against the dangers that might ensue if the predatory interests, after being cast out, should come back in disguise and unite themselves to the Executive, and through him acquire control of the Government. That is what the predatory interests did, when they came back in the livery of hypocrisy, and under false pretenses, obtained the passage of the Fed. The danger that the Country was warned against came upon us, and is shown in the long train of horrors attendant upon the affair of the traitorous and dishonest Fed.

Look around you when you leave this Chamber, and you will see evidences of it in all sides. This is an era of misery, and for the conditions that caused that misery, the Fed are fully liable.

This is an era of financed crime, and in the financing of crime, the Fed does not play the part of a disinterested spectator.

"It has been said that the draughtsman who was employed to write the text of the Fed, used a text of the Aldrich bill, because that had been drawn up by lawyers, by acceptance bankers of European origin in New York. It was a copy, in general a translation of the statues of the Riechbank, and other European central banks.

One-half million dollars was spent on the part of the propaganda organized by these bankers, for the purpose of misleading public opinion, and giving Congress the impression that there was an overwhelming popular demand for it, and the kind of currency that goes with it, namely, an asset currency, based on human debts and obligations.

Dr. H. Parker Willis had been employed by Wall Street and propagandists, and when the Aldrich measure failed-he obtained employment with Carter Glass, to assist in drawing the banking bill for the Wilson administration. He appropriated the text of the Aldrich bill. There is no secret about it, the text of the Federal Reserve Act was tainted from the first.

A few days before the bill came to a vote, Senator Henry Cabot Lodge, of Massachusetts, wrote to Senator John W. Weeks as follows:

New York City, December 17, 1913

My Dear Senator Weeks:

Throughout my public life I have supported all measures designed to take the Government out of the banking business. This bill puts the Government into the banking business, as never before in our history. The powers vested in the Federal Reserve Board seen to me highly dangerous, especially where there is political control of the Board. I should be sorry to hold stock in a bank subject to such dominations. The bill as it stands, seems to me to open the way to a vast inflation of the currency.

I had hoped to support this bill, but I cannot vote for it as it stands, because it seems to me to contain features, and to rest upon principles, in the highest degree menacing to our prosperity, to stability in business, and to the general welfare of the people of the United States.

Very Truly Yours,
Henry Cabot Lodge.

In eighteen years that have passed since Senator Lodge wrote that letter of warning, all of his predictions have come true. The Government is in the banking business as never before.

Against its will, it has been made the backer of horse thieves and card sharps, bootleggers smugglers, speculators, and swindlers in all parts of the world. Through the Fed, the riffraff of every country is operating on the public credit of the United States Government.

Meanwhile, and on account of it, we ourselves are in the midst of the greatest depression we have ever known. From the Atlantic to the Pacific, our Country has been ravaged and laid waste by the evil practices of the Fed, and the interests which control them. At no time in our history, has the general welfare of the people been at a lower level, or the minds of the people so full of despair.

Recently, in one of our States, 60,000 dwelling houses and farms were brought under the hammer in a single day. 71,000 houses and farms in Oakland County, Michigan were sold, and their erstwhile owners dispossessed. The people who have thus been driven out, are the wastage of the Fed. They are the victims of the Fed. Their children are the new slaves on the auction blocks, in the revival of the institution of human slavery.

In 1913, before the Senate Banking and Currency Committee, Mr. Alexander Lassen made the following statement: "The whole scheme of the Fed, with its commercial paper, is an impractical, cumbersome machinery, and is simply a cover to secure the privilege of issuing money; to evade payment of as much tax upon its circulation as possible, and then control, issue and maintain, instead of reducing interest rates. It will prove to the advantage of the few, and the detriment of the people. It will mean continued shortage of actual money, and further extension of credits, for when there is a shortage of money, people have to borrow at their cost."

A few days before the Fed passed, Senator Root denounced the

Fed as an outrage on our liberties. He predicted: "Long before we wake up from our dream of prosperity through an inflated currency, our gold-which alone could have kept us from catastrophe, will have vanished, and no rate of interest will tempt it to return."

The Fed Became Law The Day Before Christmas Eve, in The year 1913, and Shortly Afterwards, the German International Bankers, Kuhn, Loeb and Co. an Affiliate of The Rothschilds, Sent One of Their Partners as Its First Director.

The Fed Note is essentially unsound. It is the Worst Currency, and The Most Dangerous, That This Country Has Ever Known.

*When the proponents of the act saw that the *Democratic doctrine would not permit them to let the proposed banks issue the new currency as bank notes, they should have stopped at that. They should not have foisted that kind of currency, namely, an asset currency, on the United States Government.*

They should not have made the Government liable on the private debts of individuals and corporations, and, least of all, on the private debts of foreigners.....(end speech quotation)....all emphasis has been added.

**Democracy's transformation into "Damn-ocracy," had begun!*

The Federal Reserve, from its inception, was a for profit corporation, and the fulfillment of Mayer Rothschilds dream. (*thus the incentive for my characterization of the Fed Note, as Rothschild "Dollars."*)

Its product is that "Dollar;" its manipulation to the benefit of its banker/owners is its business; their bottom line the measure of its success; world power its ultimate goal!

Congress, by abdicating its Constitutionally mandated task of issuing the nations money and regulating its value, awarded the "Fed," the power to determine the value of our time, and the destiny of our nation.

Following World War II, US corporate business, and US corporate government, became one and the same, completing the transition of Sovereign United States, into Corporate United States.

Thus, this bankers dream materialized, and, as intended, became the vehicle of world domination, fulfilling all expectations.

American and British based corporations, through diversification and merger, expanded the scope of their products, services, and territory, thus acquiring multi-national status.

In a world of chaos, extremely weakened governments, and virtually no business structure, these corporations experienced few problems acquiring control of the worlds natural resources.

Aided by unlimited consumer demand, a burgeoning technology industry, and seemingly unlimited funds earmarked for maintaining conditions conducive to commerce, a revised version of world government British style, became world government American style; protected and maintained by American military might: World Feudalism!

The individual sovereignty of the American people was consumed by the beast, and, as was planned, vampire like attached itself to the economic throat of American commerce, exacting tribute from every transaction.

Although the designers and instigators of the Federal Reserve system, through the treasonous conduct of the nations "trusted" representatives, achieved their objective, they did not count on the absolute irresponsibility of subsequent "leaders."

This wealth harvesting system, painstakingly devised too operate like clockwork, and too be totally unintelligible to very nearly 100% of the nations citizenry as well as its leadership, was thus implanted within the US Treasury.

Even those who have acquired a proficiency in the manipulation of the system, and manage to "work the levers and shift the gears" for immense profit, possess not an inkling as to its true function, nor the intricacies of its construction.

Less than twenty years from its implantation in 1913, as previously detailed, the United States found itself in the grasp of the most sever economic depression in its history.

Our escape from this disaster was purchased with the blood of our youth, in World War II.

Emerging from the conflict into a world of devastation, the only combatant whose manufacturing capacity was not only unscathed, but much stronger than upon its entry into the war, the United States citizenry, by default, became leader, nursemaid, farmer, and healer--our currency the world standard.

The American population, from the nations infancy, has harbored neither desire nor aspiration toward either militarism, or empire; quite the contrary, after every conflict, including WWII, our military forces were greatly reduced. However, concurrent with the invasion of South Korea by North Korea, soon to be joined by Red China, we were thrust into the role of world policeman.

Democracy, capitalism, communism, and the domino effect, immediately became the buzz words of the 1950's.

The US, up to its ass in the alligators of containment of the octopus known as the USSR, found itself in no position to heed Presidents Eisenhower's warning against surrendering our economic system, to a military industrial complex.

When John Kennedy, upon assuming the office of President, surrendered our nations insurmountable military advantage over the Soviet Union, the die was cast for our current economic situation.

President Kennedy, with the implementation of his MAD doctrine, not only allowed, but actively assisted the Soviets in achieving and maintaining military parity.

The implementation of this asinine doctrine, simultaneously bestowed control of the nation to the military industrial complex/fed.

The ensuing arms race, combined with the extremely expensive technological advances in armament required of both antagonist, greatly assisted the Federal Reserve in their goal of harvesting the wealth created by past, present and future generations.

President Roosevelt, in the early 1930's had stripped the dollar, as used in domestic trade, of its gold backing, however, the dollar, when used to settle world trade accounts, was still backed by gold.

Lyndon Johnson, in the mid 1960's, *by escalating the cold war, fighting a hot one in Viet Nam, and instituting a social monstrosity known as the "Great Society" All on Credit,* inaugurated our high flying governments final approach into the bankruptcy referred to by Representative Traficant, in his 1993 speech to Congress.

We had borrowed so much money during the Kennedy/Johnson administrations, that the lenders were getting nervous, thus, when Charles DeGaulle began demanding that the United States relinquish the gold collateralizing the loans owed to France, several other nations demanded the same.

Because the national debt, even then, had escalated well beyond the point that it could by collateralized by gold, President Nixon was forced to default on redemption, or the treasury would have been emptied.

In spite of the long recognized reality, that any nation instituting paper "money" ("legal" counterfeiting) , simultaneously exposes their citizenry to the risk of Illegal counterfeiting as well, the *asset currency system*, instituted by the FED in 1913, was totally implemented.

Under this system, each Federal Reserve "dollar," is, in effect, an unquestioned "title" to a small part of the nation. With enough of them you can buy a car, a house, or a boat full of cocaine, if you so choose.

The assets of the United States, including the land mass itself, now collateralizes world trade. Yes, those same *"Rothschild Dollars,"* that our politicians now borrow in prodigious quantity from the Federal Reserve, then scatter to the winds.

In an effort to maintain the value of these assets, virtually every tree, blade of grass, and other natural resources, in the guise of environmental protection, are now being "protected," locked away by law, in order to assure its safe keeping for our " lawful" creditors.

The irony of the current situation is that via the avenue of the Federal Reserve money system, our assets are being utilized to destroy not only themselves, but our freedom, and not only through "legal" tender.

Anyone one who believes that with the state of modern technology, and the expertise available to foreign governments, that counterfeit "money" is not also backing the current terrorist problem, is living in a fantasy world!

It gets worse! Our nations mortgaged assets, fund the drug trade. Our government has devastated our economy, and destroyed our criminal justice system, fighting a "war on drugs" a "business not only facilitated by, but absolutely dependent upon Federal Reserve "money" for its very existence, *"money" collateralized by the assets of the nation.*

The money generated by this "business," just in the one hundred dollar denominated Federal Reserve notes, is so vast, that it is weighed, rather than counted.

While "American Money" has, for the last fifty years, been flowing like water to foreign governments, and facilitating organized crime, thanks to the lack of good jobs, and the depreciating value of the currency, the income of a majority of Americans has deteriorated to the point that in many households, it doesn't cover basic living expenses.

Adequate medical coverage? Your dreaming, right?

The reality is, that thanks too "Uncle Sam's" "generosity," a personal debt of over $100,000.00, is the greeting awaiting every child upon drawing his/her first breathe. *No wonder they enter the world crying.*

While a very large number of our citizenry attempt to "get by" on less than then ten dollars per hour, our already well paid "public servants" just increased their own salary, while "budgeting" four hundred billion dollars more of our common wealth, to endless debt.

Adding insult to injury, our multi-millionaire President, tosses another billion dollars per week into the bottomless pit of Iraq.

For Perspective, Lets Explore the Term FRN (Federal Reserve Note!)

If I placed a twenty dollar bill FRN on the table next to a stack of twenty true silver dollars, and told you to take your pick, which would you choose? A hint! It would take at least nine of the bills to purchase the coins!

Although both silver dollars, and one dollar federal reserve notes, are categories of currency trading side by side within the United States, and both bear the word dollar, if one will not trade evenly for the other, isn't the government complicate in deception and fraud?

The answer obviously is yes. The mystery is revealed in the term "category." The silver dollar classifies as both lawful and legal, the federal reserve note, only legal.

The definition of a dollar is found in our Bureau of Weights and Measures. As stated within the Coinage Act of 1792, our dollar is defined as 371.25 grains of 900 pure silver. Its weight was derived to exactly match in weight, the Spanish silver milled dollar, a coin which had been adopted, and was in wide use, during our nations early history. The gold dollar was then defined as one fifteenth the weight of the silver dollar or 24.75 grains of 900 pure gold.

Smaller denominations of coinage were then derived by halving the weight of the silver dollar to create the half dollar, quartering it to produce the quarter, and dividing it by 10 to produce the dime. The five cent piece was to be made of nickel, and the penny, or one cent, of copper, with weight commensurate with the intrinsic value of the metal.

When you hold a coin of either silver or gold, you hold the actual worth of metal, and its value is determined by those interested in owning it; nothing any government can do will change that fact.

Let's say that I have a 1954 Corvette (I dream big) that you have fallen in love with, so you politely ask if I would entertain an offer of $30,000.00 for the car. Repressing my first impulse, I politely, and correctly respond, dollars gold, or dollars silver.

We would then be discussing items of intrinsic value; my car, and your money, and would each be responsible for assessing the value of the items, as personally applied.

The comparison of prices actually paid for other Corvettes of the same model and condition, easily found in trade publications, would determine the value which I place upon my car.

Although the value, as inscribed upon your one ounce Gold Eagle is $50.00 US, its barter value (the price of one once of gold on the commodity exchange, plus its premium value as a coin), undoubtedly would determine the value you place on each coin.

If the deal was consummated, a barter, not a sale, of two items, each possessing equal intrinsic value as agreed by two individuals, would have taken place. The only value of the term "dollar" would have been as a common point of reference in the discussion.

Should you reply that you do not have the price asked in dollars gold or silver, but you do own a 57 Thunderbird in comparable condition, and would be interested in an even trade, then again, we are trading intrinsic value as each of us defines it, whether we value the vehicles at $100.00 or $100,000.00 each.

If the United States issued gold or silver certificates, as once was the case, then the certificate would be exchangeable for gold or silver at its face value, thus satisfying the requirement for United States money, as established by the Constitution.

Because I could exchange the paper money for the metal, you could merely count out the face value of the bills to equal the posted price for the car, I would assign the title to you, and a sale would have taken place.

You may then drive the car home, park it in you garage, wait for it to appreciate in value, and never drive it again, if you so choose. By the same token, I can put the certificates in a safety deposit box, and, because that which they represent is guaranteed to meet the definition of US money, I may hold them for as long as I choose; never worrying about losing the value I placed on my Corvette.

NOT TRUE OF FEDERAL RESERVE NOTES.

A Federal Reserve Note neither possess intrinsic value, nor does it represent anything possessing intrinsic value! Neither does it maintain a stable value, nor does the government guarantee its value.

Contrarily, Federal Reserve currency begins to lose its value from the moment of printing, thus, any individual or company exposes themselves to risk immediately upon its acceptance.

That risk is embodied by the term inflation, the more currency printed, the less it is worth!

Lets briefly return to the Corvette. Lets say that you purchased the car to satisfy a desire dating back into your high school days when it was produced by General Motors.

You now own an SUV, that, with roll up windows and air conditioning is considerably more comfortable, so the Vette is just parked in your garage, and, because no more are being built, daily increasing in value.

Lets say for arguments sake, that you had convinced me to sell the car for Federal Reserve Notes rather than gold. Having no immediate need for the cash, I just put the bills in a safety deposit box as a rainy day fund. Five years pass; you proudly drive the Vette occasionally and really enjoy the compliments and admiring stares.

At times an admirer will attempt to persuade you to sell the car with some very good offers. $46,000.00~~ $50,000.00 and with every offer you congratulate yourself on the good deal you got when you purchased it, and you know, because there will never be another one made, that it will never lose its value.

I on the other hand, finding myself in need of the money in the cash box, discover, to my dismay, that because the Federal Reserve has printed billions more paper notes, that the money I received for the car, has lost half its value.

The truth than strikes me that I in fact, netted only $15,000.00 for

the Corvette, and, that if I retain the Notes for an extended period of time, that eventually, I, in reality, will have given it away.

As I realize that had I continued to demand gold, and had put it in the cash box, that because more of it is still being mined, that it perhaps would not have gained much value, however, it would certainly have retained that which it originally possessed; I can do nothing other than regret my decision. I then pick up a trade journal, and thinking of the Corvette which I had once owned, read the prices that they now command when someone foolishly decides sell one, and cry.

If the President decides to wage war against Iraq for example, and informs we the citizens that the estimated cost of its prosecution, rebuilding, extended deployment, and humanitarian assistance, over a ten year period, will total between three and four trillion dollars, to be immediately funded with new taxes, neither he, nor the war would be very popular.

To ward of a financial depression caused by the new taxes, the Federal Reserve must print additional currency against the value of current assets. The currency is introduced into the economy by way of contracts to multinational corporation, and are then distributed as pay checks, as well as by other means; which, in turn, raises the cost of everything from a can of corn, to a new car, in real time, in a word, INFLATION!

Just the terms "increased taxation" and "inflation" evokes a very negative attitude toward politicians, their desire to avoid it is therefore quite obvious. Too this end, the cost of war is financed, as are most pet social programs.

Just like your credit card, the only repayment requirements, are regular installments on the accruing interest, and, as applied to government, the principle may be increased seemingly indefinitely.

Government loans are collateralized by the nations assets, and, as things now stand, the responsibility for their redemption, *is transferred to generations yet unborn.*

Every bomb that ripped a building apart in Baghdad, and every promise made to rebuild it, committed more American assets.

Just the interest payments on the existing trillions of dollars debt is unimaginable, yet, and I reiterate--our "Damn-ocratic Representatives" just "budgeted" a four hundred billion dollar increase, excluding the cost of the war, requiring President Bush to submit a request for additional funding of almost ninety billion dollars!

Every man or woman who fought the war, will be refunding their wages many times over, just to pay the forever accruing interest, on the seemingly endless debt, as well as buying every bomb, bullet, and gallon of fuel.

Those Who Rendered the Ultimate Sacrifice, Will Lie Eternally in a Mortgaged Grave.

Government, as with any enterprise, when cost exceeds it value over an extended period of time, and the citizens are no longer willing to supply the extra revenue, bankruptcy is inevitable.

Too continue to operate by pyramiding debt, and multiplying interest load, does nothing more than extend, and exacerbate the inevitable to our children and grandchildren, ad infinitum.

Adding insult to injury, Lyndon Johnson, shortly after being sworn in as President, ordered the existing silver coins to be called in, scrapped, and clad coins issued in their place; additionally, all silver certificates were to be exchanged for Federal Reserve notes.

The last vestiges of its money, thus, presence of our former Republic, became the first victim of our "Damn-ocratic" Government.

The Nations Multimillion Ounce Silver Reserve, Has Subsequently Vanished!

During the 12 years the Reagan/Bush administrations held the reigns of government, the United States transitioned from largest creditor, to largest debtor nation.

Taking maximum advantage of the federal governments tax and give away policies, nations that were once debtors, are now creditors. These policies are not only unfair to domestic manufacturers, but have driven many out of business, or to foreign shores.

What is so strange however, is the fact that state governors and legislators, although facing local tax revolts and balanced budget mandates, *for some reason, cannot associate the national monetary policy, and huge debt load, with their financial woes.*

The American people, while committing our children to the task of world policeman, have been robbed blind, and are in the final stages of being pauperized, by a centuries old criminal syndicate, in the guise of International Bankers!

Resources which should have remained within the states, were, and are, being stolen by means of the federal income tax; thus, instead of fixing bridges, roads and schools, they are added to assets of the Federal Reserve, (International Bankers) as interest on the national debt.

DECLARATION OF INDEPENDENCE

The American government, when instituted according to the Declaration of Independence, is dedicated to the protection of rights inherent within the Laws of Nature, and Natures God.

To the author of the Declaration of Independence, the absence of individual right to Life, Freedom, and Property, relegated birth to the status of an exercise in futility; he reasoned therefore, that they must be an endowment of our Creator.

The lack of perfection in the personal life of Thomas Jefferson, its author, has recently been employed for the purpose of diminishing the perception of his devotion to the cause of liberty, and the dedication of his life toward that end.

The besmirching of a good mans name, and the belittling of his character, directed toward the devaluation of his courage and achievements, is disgusting.

I can't tell you who won baseballs World Series, footballs Super Bowl, nor even the names of the contenders, however, I long ago committed the following words of Thomas Jefferson, My Hero, to memory.

"We hold these truths to be self evident, that all men are created equal; that they are endowed by their Creator with certain unalienable rights; that among these, are Life, Liberty, and the pursuit of Happiness. That to secure these rights, governments are instituted among men, deriving their just powers from the consent of the governed."

No, they did not immediately result in perfect government, nor instant freedom for all, however, in my opinion: They Express the Exalted Status of Mankind--The Created Image, To the Level Intended by Our Creator.

The founders of our nation, as are we, were bound by the reality,

knowledge and technology of their time, and could build no better government, than that which was possible, under their existing circumstances.

Henry Ford did not build a perfect automobile, Wilbur and Orville Wright a perfect airplane, nor Thomas Edison a perfect light bulb, none of these men were perfect; they were all human, with the attendant frailties; yet our current life styles, greatly indebted to their endeavors, were not diminished in the least.

These fifty six words, a simple recognition of truth, sent shock waves throughout every kingdom, and created trepidation within every crowned head of Europe.

By redefining its source, they redirected the power of government; however, a very small portion of that truth, was then, or, two centuries later, is yet realized in any nation.

In any case, today, as history is either being re-written, selectively interpreted, or simply not taught in US schools, the debt owed Jefferson, and the other founders of our nation, is being trivialized, and their insight into the reality of human purpose, hidden under a cloud of negative propaganda.

Thomas Jefferson, by recognizing the sovereign status of the individual, thus, dedicated any following government too the protection of that principle.

At the conclusion of the War for Independence, the accomplishment of these goals was already being fulfilled by state, or colonial constitutions, consequently, *central government enjoyed no assumption of an inherent right too exist !*

Contrarily, the citizens had to be sold on its need, before the first word concerning its structure, was even uttered; thus, the Articles of Confederation, a document conferring virtually no power, Was a Very Tough Sell!

Consequently, as borne out by the Federalist Papers, our present Constitution did not materialize from out of the clear blue! The result of an attempt to amend The Articles..., not institute new government, it faced an even greater challenge than had they, and was only approved with the imposition of sever limitations.

Under these circumstances, the resulting government, possessing no assumed right to exist, certainly possessed no mandate favoring any philosophical or religious agenda, in fact, quite the opposite.

The much ballyhooed propaganda of the United States being a "Christian" nation is just that, propaganda. There is nothing in either the Federalist Papers, Declaration of Independence, nor the Constitution, that even hints at this assertion.

Quite the contrary! The Declaration... is dedicated too the Laws of Nature and Natures God, and The Constitution to individual thought, speech, and actions, the fulfillment of principles espoused within The Declaration of Independence.

We each, as the result of natural, individual--not mass creation, are indebted too neither church nor government for our empowerment; contrarily, both church, and government, are beholding to the individual for their very existence.

While we do possess the right to participate in the Christian religion, we also possess the right to participate in any other religion, or none at all; the most basic of individual rights.

Although its writing and approval spanned several years, our Constitution may be read in about twenty minutes by those possessing even a rudimentary education. The basic document was approved with the stipulation that it be immediately amended for the purpose of clarification, thus, ten amendments spelled out the philosophy under which the Constitution had been written.

Our nations founders, in no uncertain terms, with the tenth amendment, by specifically stating that any power not specifically given to the federal government remained with either the citizens or the state, simultaneously reduced the authority of the central government.

However, its mandated purpose, that of the securing of life, liberty, and the rights of property, to every citizen of the nation, although channeled, bestowed tremendous latitude to its awesome power.

This ten amendment addendum, written in the language of the average citizen, came to be known as the Bill of Rights. Its intended purpose, that of interpretive aid of the Constitution, is very well served.

At the time they were written, there was concern among the delegates that the amendments would be construed as limitations upon sovereignty, rather than as merely specific examples of universal rights, thus, the very specific, declarative language of the tenth.

Even with that language, and its attendant history, today their concerns are proving very valid.

As an example: The unrelenting assault upon the Second Amendment, extending to the argument that its repeal would eliminate the principle, totally ignores the statement that: any power not specifically delegated to the federal government, remains with the state or the individual--*the concept upon which the Constitution itself was ratified.*

Does this argument simply display ignorance of the language, as well as intent of purpose of the document to which their oath of office is dedicated; or does it display arrogant perjury?

Which is worse; self imposed ignorance, or willful contempt of the trust with which they have been honored?

Because the Terms are Mutually Exclusive, A Democratic *Republic*, is an Impossible Concept!

With a democratic system available to them, why did our nations founders bother writing the Constitution?

I'll ask one of them: Mr. Madison, why didn't you just create a government of majority rule, we know that it was considered? His reply, per, the Federalist papers:

"Democracies have ever been spectacles of turbulence and contention; have ever been found incompatible with personal security or the rights of property, and have in general, been as brief in their duration, as they have been violent in their death."

This statement was short and to the point; words of wisdom which have been with us for over two centuries; an admonition which we apparently do not believe worth pondering, and certainly not worth following.

Mr. Madison's statement recognizes the folly, and anticipates the answers to questions that cut to the very heart of direct democracy. Questions, which if not answered before the fact, will, without doubt destroy the government of any nation in which it is enacted, after the fact. This is being proven even now, in the nation which he helped to create.

In a democratic nation, what percentage of the electorate should be required to empower the government to confiscate Private property? Private Industry? Private land? Is fifty-one percent sufficient, or, should the figure be at least fifty-five?

Perhaps we should employ a sliding scale determined by individual rank of importance, i.e, fifty-one percent for guns and automobiles, and fifty-five for houses, land, and certain business.

Of course industries considered critical to the nations welfare,

such as communications, transportation, and health care, should definitely require only a whisker over fifty percent.

How About Our Civil Liberties? Our Time? Our Money?

In the final analysis, does the initial figure really matter; <u>it can always be changed by the will of the majority, or redefined by "The Court," Right,?</u>

How unified or stable would you expect the society of this nation, state, or city to be?

For these, and the following reasons, our nations government was created a Constitutional Republic; governed by citizen representatives, chosen by majority ballot; however; *delegating no power not possessed by each individual voter, nor specifically invested in the office by that Constitution.*

Succinctly stated: *A democratic selection process, does not necessarily create, a Democratic state.*

While compromise is necessary in the implementations of decisions and policies surrounding its Lawful Power, the *areas not specifically delegated , are to be not only free of compromise at the governmental level, but, are not even to be topics of discussion.*

The purpose of these limitations, is of course, to protect the sanctity of our personal lives from intrusion, and our personal property from confiscation, by majority vote of our fellow citizens.

However, although we all enjoy the freedoms it protects, because the Constitution blocks the way to things we each desire to accomplish through government, many of us are all too willing to not only allow, but to actively encourage our officers and representatives to disregard its limitations.

This practice now saturates our political and societal processes; polarizing our citizenry, and mocking our nations founding principles.

In a nation comprised entirely of sovereign individuals, how did its founders acquire the co-operation required to create a self governing society?

The answer: They didn't. They were wise enough to recognize that a society was beyond their reach; a government however was possible, but only by overcoming the influences of previous societies, based upon class position, and aristocratic domination.

Although we speak of society, actually our culture is composed of many interacting societies. While one person might find it advantageous to belong to a segment composed of opera aficionados, a country music person might consider it dire punishment; the same is true in regard to the various religions.

These circumstances dictated a framework of government in which the various factions of society could interact as a network, thus, creating the whole.

The goal was achieved only after years of diligent work and compromise, and was possible only by limiting the power of government, to the coding into law, universally accepted standards of conduct common to all persons sharing its benefits.

It wasn't perfect to be sure, however, a mere acknowledgment of the current division created by the various societal factions, in their quest for sufficient governmental power to control the whole of society, reveals the fact that the task could not be accomplished today.

To achieve these goals, government cannot attempt to be all things to each citizen, but must strive to be the same thing to every citizen, an entity devoid of partisanship.

What our ancestors could devise however, they could not implement. Their government consisted of one giant partisanship, consisting of the white male; a government which immediately began to self destruct.

From the conclusion of the Civil War, each fragment of the disintegrating social structure labored to secure its individual identity. Following the Second World War, they were actively joined in their effort by the government.

This process has been accompanied by strife, and a certain amount of turmoil, however, *establishment of the individual sovereignty of every citizen, was obviously a prerequisite to the voluntary subordination of a portion of it, to a new society based upon equal justice.*

The process created an entirely new political structure.

As ingredients of power and sources of wealth, new partisanships have become refined commodities; our institutions of government devoted market places; our elected representatives, master salesmen; and the various factions of society, eager customers.

Thus, United States the Nation, through government, was transformed into United States the business, with Washington DC, its brothel.

Like exotic animals in a game preserve, a treasure trove of potential partisanships lay just out of reach, protected by Supreme Law, from the purview of elected representatives.

A piece of paper and an oath however, has not stopped representatives of government, anymore than a law and a fence stops any dedicated poacher.

Because they were placed within the reserve by contract, many have proven especially lucrative. Gun control as an example, like a trophy grizzly, continues to bring great rewards to

political poachers.

How do we recognize a legitimate claim, from a poached partisanship? Very easily!

The Concept of The Declaration of Independence, Creates Only Winners!

Thus, if by honoring a "right" of one individual, another's right is denied, *thereby creating a loser,* in all likelihood a poached partisanship was involved.

This is true, because upon election to a public office, representatives acquire a responsibility to represent a constituency; *this constituency consist of every citizen within their jurisdiction.*

Unlike a democracy, where the rule of the mob, over rides the rights of the individual, in *a Republic the rights of the individual are sacrosanct, and are to be protected by government.*

If to " honor " elicit Partisanships, requires that a representative dishonor their oath of office guaranteeing each person *Constitutional Representation,* then that action constitutes criminal misconduct--unfortunately, a common practice.

Any candidate running for office on a promise to represent one person or group, at the expense of another, or, in violation of the Constitution, is revealing their true character.

In a campaign to " reform " government, various fraternal orders of professional politicians (parties) dedicated to the "election" (sale) of their members, now routinely employ illicit Partisanships as the favored means of fomenting hostility, all part of a divide and conquer strategy.

As this strategy is rewarded with enthusiastic response by myriad factions, a stable, harmoniously functioning society becomes an impossible dream.

The turmoil created by the various factions in this "reformation by confrontation" collusion, has diminished the public perception of their integrity; cast doubts upon their respective credibility; and, by destroying the foundation of government, de-stabilized it.

As conditions within our nation continue to validate Mr. Madison critique of democratic government, perhaps an analysis of our brief experience with it will tell us why he has proven so successful a prophet.

To begin with, *Nothing Materializes from Thin Air,* everything, including government, must have a source.

A system of majority rule, is predicated upon the principle that a plurality of consent, justifies the use of government force to achieve a political objective.

This might makes right ideology derives its power from the "legalization" of conduct, which, if perpetrated by the individual citizen, would be condemned and prosecuted as reprehensible.

Government Empowered, By Delegation Of Authority!

It is certainly no secret that regardless of the name with which it is labeled, our Republic was designed, per the Declaration of Independence, to function as a form of *self government, whose sole source of power, derives from the consent of each individual,* thus the name, *<u>Collective Self Government.</u>*

Under This System, Government is Entitled Only to the Authority Possessed by Each Individual.

That Which Doesn't Exist Individually, Cannot Be Delegated Collectively!

This barrier to majority rule, represents the stabilizing factor necessary to a peaceful, productive, governed society.

The Right To Keep And Bear Arms, Is Applicable Only Within The Context Of The Collective! Right?

Sure It Is!

Absent the guaranteed right of defense of either life, or property, *where is either advantage, or incentive, to either civilized behavior, or government ?*

After all, *the endowment of life, and liberty, absent the accompanying endowment of the right and means of defending either, would amount to a worthless gift from our creator; would it not?*

Why then, would anyone in their right mind; facing circumstances under which they could be required to either kill or be killed; create a government, under which they would relinquish the means of self defense?

Thus, the principle that each individual was justified in employing any means at his or her disposal, for the purpose of protecting their life, as well as their property, made perfect sense to our nations founders.

This principle, when accompanied by the fact that the action was to be examined, and either condemned or justified in a court of common law, by a jury of their peers, became the universally accepted principle, upon which a government could be established.

This sovereign right, secured by the Supreme Law of the Land, established an atmosphere conducive to trust, at least to the point that the founding citizenry of the nation, felt comfortable enough to *selectively defer portions of their individual rights,* to the proposed government.

However, common sense dictates, that authority bestowed to

selected individuals through the deferral of rights, is itself mitigated by restrictions, natural limitations, and common sense application.

Thus, we, the current citizenry, acting as government, centralize, organize, and thus magnify our individual power to act against those violating universally accepted prohibitions.

A plurality of votes however, bestows no authority not specifically enumerated, **and thus, may be in no way construed, as the enhancement of non-existing authority.**

Whether perpetrated by either a lone individual or a collective of millions, theft is theft, and murder, murder, and has been since the beginning of time!

Trust Is the Glue Which Binds a Free Society.

Because self government of the collective, must derive from self governing individuals, behavior, if abhorrent to the individual, must also remain abhorrent within the collective.

Just as society enjoys the right to expect the individual to honor the trust invested in them, the individual enjoys the reciprocal right of being granted trust by society, until they, by their actions, prove unworthy of that trust.

Society, merely for convenience or desire, cannot exempt the collective, nor those formulating and enforcing the law, from that law, without also exempting the individual.

Regardless of the Damn-ocratic approval percentage, because the law derives from authority which doesn't exist, it becomes a criminal act by society.

After all the I's have been dotted, T's crossed, and the guns of law enforcement used to finalize the proceedings:

Theft remains theft and murder--murder:

Society's credibility, thus its viability is compromised:

The individual assumes the same "might makes right" as well as the "end justifies the means" attitude:

And the law of the jungle, is again the law of the land!

Thus the old truism, "Justice "Cost Money, How Much Of It Can You Afford" is still alive and well, in the USA!

A Violation Of Trust!

Just as a criminal act by the individual results in status transformation, the same is true as it relates to society.

As an example.

The immediate intent of supporters of a gun control law , is the creation of an inanimate "criminal."

Their ultimate intent however, is the criminalization, of the "offense," of refusing to render unquestioned obedience to their authority, thereby reducing their fellow citizens, even those possessing unblemished citizenship, to the status of criminal.

This evokes and interesting question! When a criminal is created by legislation, is it the targeted citizenry, or the creators of the legislation?

In a true Republican nation,* in accordance with a Supreme law guaranteeing each state a *true Republican government,* a *true Republican party,* would be vociferously contending that: *Only the intentional actions of a sovereign individual, may be deemed criminal, while pointing out, that the creation of criminal objects, is the hallmark of totalitarian government.

As represented by the enemies, in every war in which we have participated, anything may be classified as criminal, including,

within our own nation, the education of Negroes.

Any elected official who so advocates, by promoting the creation of a criminal society, create criminals of themselves.

If failure to exercise individual self government constitutes a crime against society, necessarily resulting in the loss of individual sovereignty, then *the stripping of benefits indigenous of individual sovereignty, by means of legislation, constitutes a criminal act by society.*

It thus follows, that if the penalty for individual breach of trust is the loss of respect by society, then the opposite is also true.

In an American society governed in accordance with common sense, not to mention the principles espoused within the Declaration of Independence, as well as the Constitution, *The Criminalization of Inanimate Objects, Is An Impossibility!*

By charging citizens with guilt by association with; possession of; or proximity too, an inanimate "criminal," i.e drugs, alcohol and perhaps guns; allowing the charge too constitute proof ; the inanimate "criminal" the sole necessary witness ; with no facts in evidence, unlawful intent is assumed; all With Judiciary Complicity, due process has thus become a farce.

Presto! The debased criminal justice system, as it now exist, has itself been transformed into a criminal institution, and justice rendered extinct.

Every unlawful act, whether by the individual, or by representative of government, is replete with consequences.

When legislative law and language, contradicts common sense, as well as common language, there is something drastically wrong with the law, as well as those who enact, and enforce it.

We the citizens, in the absence of the required education, are

legally, though unlawfully bound by the admonition that: ignorance of the law is no excuse.

Does it then make sense, that individuals, acting through oath, in the name of government, and many times educated in the law, are not so bound?

Thus, if those acting unlawfully under the auspices of government, are not required to suffer those consequences, then the repercussion are transferred, also unlawfully, to the collective.

It is becoming increasingly apparent, that as surely as the advantages of obeying the rules of society, as proclaimed by sovereign law, is destroyed, chaos becomes inevitable.

How much farther must our society deteriorate, before we began too understand that every time we utilize the shield of government too condone the breaking of inherent law, we tear another hole in the fabric of our society?

How can we condemn our children for their lack of respect for the common laws of the land, while displaying our own contempt for these laws by disregarding them through government?

The Majestic Power of the Press.

If in the absence of trust, and in the midst of chaos, those in power assume the authority to control the population by force of arms, or, economic coercion, the power of the people will divide between those determined to preserve the Constitution, and others for respect of the power and prestige of elected representation, although illicitly wielded.

The power of the press, will, in all likelihood, be used to exhort and justify the use of institutional force, against those maintaining respect for the limitations imposed on government by the Constitution.

How and why are these destructive procedures being perpetuated?

The answer is summed up in two words, Money and Power.

Our Declaration of Independence states, that all just power of government, is derived from consent of the govern.

This is true only because the means of withholding that consent exist. In reality, Republican government, by design, operates one level above anarchy!

Think not? Then explain the specific, individual right to weapons.

Consequently, consent must be sought, obtained, and maintained by policies designed to confer just, uniform treatment to every citizen, or, we must be simultaneously educated to accept the status of subservience to government, and the desirability of surrendering the means of withholding our consent.

This wedge of contention is now being driven between our citizenry by a mass " news " media, owned by extremely wealthy families, with a vested interest in retaining a government dominated by money.

In a "Damn-ocracy," the Press Is Mightier Then the Sword!

Both money and power may be acquired and maintained in greater quantity, with less risk and even pseudo honor, when concealed under a cloak of propaganda. Those who control the means of mass communication, thus become king makers.

This is however, a qualified statement, the qualifier is credibility. Propaganda tends to play fast and loss with the truth, and the "news media " in their desire to influence societal development, has unabashedly editorialized "the news," in an

effort to affect a contrived reality.

Is there any question, that our thoughts, as well as our desires are being directed, and that we are, to a great extent, being offered our "choice " of purchased, packaged, and merchandised politicians?

According to our vote, or lack thereof, one of these "chosen " few becomes a part of our "leadership," and they in turn are influenced by the polls to "give" us what we have been educated to won't, even if it requires taking it from someone else.

This is "Corporate Damn-ocracy" in action, the reality of majority rule.

Even in its limited form, it has compromised our government's ability to govern. They are however, no longer preaching to semi-literate hicks, with limited access to information, this is reflected in their declining ratings and influence.

Various versions of "truth," transmitted by computer, is now dissolving the dark habitat necessary for lies and manipulated information to proliferate.

The invention of the printing press, was, in my opinion, the single most important development in human evolution within the last thousand years.

The fact that the human race was designed to function and prosper by the division of labor is beyond dispute, however, the first and foremost requisite of collective labor, must be the compiling of collective information, acquired through individual experiences.

The accumulation and dissemination of this information, instituted the link which has, and will continue, to magnify the importance of each unique bit and piece; in this context, the computer is simply the latest progeny of the printing press.

The Reality of Unavoidable Evolution.

Few thinking citizens will dispute the fact that our society, as it existed only a few years ago, is dead, and is being rapidly interred.

Should the mainstream media desire to avoid their own burial, then they must begin viewing the world as it actually exist today, envision it as it is likely to exist tomorrow, and quit trying to perpetuate a dead or dying reality, by "spinning " the news.

Although they lobbied relentlessly for government control of both guns and health care, and, the "polls" we were informed, indicated that the American people overwhelmingly favored both policies, the truth was revealed at the next election.

Again, a vast majority of Americans recognized theft, even Damn-ocratic theft, still to be theft.

This is not a new tactic! For eons "peace" has been maintained by dictatorial governments, by "educating" the citizens to accept something less than justice, and resorting to lethal public punishment of resistors, as an example to potential ones.

However, regardless of how it is packaged, nothing can match the allure of either justice or freedom, once either has been either recognized or experienced.

So while the punishment inflicted at Waco as an example, might deter some inclined to resist government decree, it also created a vast number of enemies, and strengthened our resolve, to resist similar action at all cost.

A Peaceful "Damn-ocracy" Is Impossible, Within an Armed Populace.

Because "Damn-ocracy" requires control, unquestioned obedience to "authority," and the ability to take, or control private property by government decree, common sense dictates

that the first property to be taken, must be private weapons, thus the "crime bill, " and later the "Patriot Act."

Although these masterpieces of legislation made a mockery of the Constitution, for the foregoing reasons they were demanded by world financial cartels, proposed by their purchased lackeys in both major political parties, and " managed " into existence, primarily by several very powerful newspaper syndicates, and television networks.

In a nutshell, they set the stage, provide the process, and determine the penalties, for violations of martial law. They give teeth to presidential orders issued by John Kennedy, orders which have been enacted into law to create FEMA, and has given birth to the "Homeland Security" behemoth.

The nations financial situation well be in another chapter, therefore the following affords nothing more than a very brief view.

Beginning in December 1913, our " Damn-ocracy " has been controlled by the Federal Reserve banking system, by means of currency manipulation. This is the only means by which any "Damn-ocracy" can survive even temporarily.

It has allowed our elected representatives to buy the votes necessary to maintain a stable constituency, and when necessary, to rig election results.

The national debt represents the expanding cost of these votes, and the willingness of our current representatives to mortgage the future of generations yet unborn, reveals the corrupting nature of "Damn-ocratic" politics.

This practice is both unethical an unlawful, and the chaos within our society, is merely the down payment of misery accompanying James Madison's predicted fate of "Damn-ocratic" government.

Forces already unleashed, and impossible to stop, will invite the very drastic solution of enforced " peace. " If/when, martial law is enforced in accordance with these laws, and under these agencies, the local police, as well as the state National Guard, become de-facto federal police, a terrifying possibility.

The "crime bill," was enacted as "sleeper legislation" in preparation for this eventuality. It became law, with the full knowledge and admission by the sponsoring Senator, Ms. Fienstine of California, that most of it was unconstitutional-- her sentiment was " Let's enact it anyway and let them take it to court."

Is this disrespect for law not the same thought process common to the young thief, murderer, and drive by shooter?

If a group of these unprincipled people form in our inner cities they are derided, condemned as gang members, and become subjects of police power.

How then does lack of respect for Supreme Law, and the willingness to perjure personal oaths, translate as respectable in an "august" body of government, and contemptible in a gang in which the oath to law is not required?

The answer is easy, it doesn't. Except in the numbers of citizens impacted, the setting constitutes the only differentiating aspect.

Beyond question, the Constitution, not the government, must be destroyed, if the planned New World Order dictatorship is to be implemented.

So long as it remains even marginally effective, it posses a fatal threat to some very well laid plans for our future. This, and other "sleeper" legislation has been enacted over the years, with full knowledge that it could not be immediately implemented, however, it is pointed, like a knife at the heart of our nation, much of it directed toward the creation of Federal criminals.

Therefore it's not the content of "the law" that is important, but the very fact of its existence. Was its purpose the infliction of the fatal blow to the Constitution, with the approval of a majority of our duped, "Damn-cratic" politicians? Perhaps!

In any event, it provides a cloak of precedent setting legality, for blatant, unlawful acts of representative intrusion, into areas specifically denied them by that document.

The compromising by debate, of subjects specifically forbidden by Supreme Law, leapfrogs the concept of obedience, and instead derives a consensus of degree, to which it will be disregarded, thus demonstrating overt contempt for the Constitution.

Much of this chapter has been centered around, and many of my conclusions based, upon the terms "legal" and "lawful," the final few paragraphs, brings this into focus!

There exist, hidden under a mountain of law books, a little known opinion which promises to de-rail this very well conceived conspiracy.

This judicial time bomb may be found in the Sixteenth American Jurisprudence, Second Edition, Section 177. quote:

" The general misconception is, that any statute passed by legislators bearing the appearance of law, constitutes the law of the land. The U.S. Constitution is The Supreme Law of The Land, and any statute, to be valid, must be in agreement.

It is impossible for both the Constitution and a law violating it to be valid; one must prevail.

This is succinctly stated as follows: the general rule is that an unconstitutional statute, though having the form and name of law, is in reality no law, but is wholly void, and ineffective for any purpose; since unconstitutionality dates from the time of its enactment, and not merely from the date of the decision so

branding it.

An unconstitutional law, in legal contemplation, is as inoperative as if it had never been passed. Such a statute leaves the question that it purports to settle just as it would be had the statue not been enacted.

Since an unconstitutional law is void, the general principles follow, that it imposes no duties, confers no rights, creates no office, bestows no authority on anyone, affords no protection, and justifies no acts performed under it.

A void act cannot be legally consistent with a valid one. An unconstitutional law cannot operate to supersede any existing valid law. Indeed, insofar as a statue runs counter to the fundamental law of the land, it is superseded thereby.

No one is bound to obey an unconstitutional law, and no courts are bound to enforcement it. close quote. (all emphasis, in every form added.)

A statement with many long years of lawful, as well as legal standing, it is well past the time, that this masterpiece of judicial common sense, be elevated to the pedestal upon which it belongs. This statement, in unequivocal language, states that all existing proven law, takes precedence over any part of any new law.

At its face value, this opinion states that any existing legislation, to be superseded immediately by new legislation, must be revoked, and the new inserted in its place. It then must meet Constitutional challenge!

Because this procedure is not followed, our " Damn-ocratic," system of contradictory law, serves as the playground for an army of expenses lawyers, many acting in concert as predators, their hapless fellow citizens their prey.

This opinion turns upside down, the present policy of enforcing

legislation until it has been challenged, and a court decision reached. Instead of the burden of proof falling on the challenger to prove unconstitutionality after enforcement, the burden is transferred to the legislature to prove constitutionality before enforcement.

Under a just system of government, this is the correct procedure.

As demonstrated according to the Congressional record itself, the crime bill was enacted under a cloud of suspicion of its constitutionality, even by those enacting it, and now the "Patriot Act" is under fire, even in the halls of the "Damn-ocratic" Congress!

If the nation was being governed under the Constitution, this, court opinion, endows each individual citizen with the right to disregard the entire legislation; furnishes the ammunition to support our action; and arms us with libraries full of precedent setting decisions.

This simply means that Congress passed, and the President signed, legislation which "lawfully" has no validity until it has been approved by the United States Supreme Court; a legislative time bomb few people have read, and even fewer understand.

"Lawfully," no person may be charged in court for disobeying any provision within the law, nor for resisting attempts to enforce provisions within it, for which previous contradictory law exists.

Contrarily, no law enforcement officer, from the attorney general down, acquires any authority under the law until it has been approved by the Supreme Court.

If not, why not? The statement contains absolutely no ambiguity, and its language certainly testifies to the fact that it was written to rescue the common citizen, from the clutches of oppressive law.

Contrary to current practices, it declares that the law itself, if challenged, must be proven valid (Supreme Court Opinion) in the court in which it is presented, before it can be applied to the challenger.

It takes no legal genius to recognize the fact that potentially, the current status of the " crime bill " creates a state of hostility between the law abiding citizens, and every police officer.

Constitutionality aside, it still leaves the legal problem of informing the citizens as to its content.

Because of the contradictory nature of the new law, and the position of the court that " ignorance of the law is no excuse " we must demand that the law, in its entirety, with legal interpretation of every article, clause, paragraph and sub-paragraph, be made available to every citizen upon whom it potentially affects .(every citizen)

These "crime bills" are further evidence that our last two generations, have, without doubt, been living under a "Damn-ocratic" government, constructed on a foundation of perpetually unstable, arbitrary, and situationally interpreted law; the results are focused in the headlines of our daily newspapers, and the lead in of our television news.

The culprit we are told is an outmoded Constitution which must be constantly re-interpreted. To a degree this is true. The Constitution was far from perfect, however, another aspect of the truth is that we have been blinded by propaganda, and are attributing the failure of forty years of "Damn-ocratic" Socialism, to deficiencies of the principals espoused by our nation's founders through the Constitution.

A majority of this document was based upon principles of natural law which needs no interpretation. Which, sans re-interpretation, commands respect, and presents few opportunities for personal aggrandizement.

The flaws were limited to its failure to extend the protection of human rights to every person regardless of race, creed, color or gender; flaws long since corrected by both legislation and court decisions.

No better system could be intentionally devised, then the contradictory law which has been written under philosophical departure from basic principles through re-interpretation, to destroy a nation from within.

By breeding chaos, confusion, and instability, not only is the perception of need for the current corrupt system enhanced, but additional opportunities for expanding the scope of illicit power and wealth, by those adept at manipulating that law is spawned.

With the signing of the Federal Reserve Act in December of 1913, President Woodrow Wilson embraced corporate government, thereby OFFICIALLY divorcing our elected governors, from the restraints imposed by the Constitution.

From that moment, The United States has been ruled by corporate policy, as determined by The Federal Reserve, and implemented by the elected government, with statutes bearing the color of law!

THE DECLARATION OF INDEPENDENCE, DOES NOT EQUAL DAMNOCRACY!

THE AMERICAN PEOPLE WERE CONQUERED!

The governmental power necessary to ensure the rights of sovereignty to every citizen, regardless of sex, creed, or religion, per the Declaration of Independence, is now the instrument of subjugation to that government.

The vast majority of citizens do not recognize the fact that our nation was united by military conquest. The Civil War, according to the words of Lincoln, was not to for the purpose of freeing the slaves, but to preserve the union.

The advocates of the principle of states rights lost the war, the advocates of the power of central government won!

While the war established the legitimate principle of the responsibility of our form of government to be the legal protection of individual rights for all citizens: unfortunately, in the process it also re-established the principle of inherent governmental power, substituting delegated authority, with assumed rights, thus spawning a new breed of politician.

Why have we forgotten the legal looting of the former Confederate states by these political scavengers in the guise of "administrators?" Although this "carpetbagger" period was of relatively short duration, the affects lasted for at least two generations; their study was still part of the curriculum in my schools days.

Today, the name, as well as the deeds, appear to have been wiped from our collective memories, perhaps so overshadowed by the civil rights movement that they simply became inconsequential.

Regardless of the reason, the nation is currently experiencing the greatest ramifications of the outcome of the war in our

history, ramifications threatening our very sovereignty.

The Constitution Restored, Was Not the Constitution Suspended!

Suspension of the Constitution, as well as the right of Habeas Corpus, resulted in nation wide rule by martial law. The reality is, it has not been totally lifted too this day.

In the early 1940's, the criticism of government policy could get you a prison sentence. Today: indefinite, incommunicado incarceration, based upon nothing more than accusation, with total deprivation of due process.

Think, and ask yourself the question: What condition existed immediately following the War for Independence? The Answer: Total Right of Individual Sovereignty! Our national government began on a blank sheet of paper.

The purpose for the war was fulfilled; it was then and there a reality; there was no national governmental structure. The only real restraint on the freeman, was the inherent moral code, or the lack thereof, within the individual.

For the first time in recent history, a sovereign people, created a sovereign government; a government founded upon a Constitution, which, if interpreted as written, is clearly intended to be applied to the government, not the citizenry!

When thusly applied, as reinforced by its Tenth Amendment, any jurisdiction, or application, not specifically enumerated, is to be off limits to the elected representatives; as acknowledged by oath, prior to their assuming the duties, to which they were elected.

MY HOW THINGS CHANGE

When the Constitution was restored, the Federal Government, and the officials staffing the offices, assumed the rights of authority, inherent of conquest. Although the words were unchanged, it began to be interpreted in accordance with British Maritime Law, that is to say, martial law.

Due to this one hundred eighty degree change of application, the citizenry were stripped of sovereignty, and the officers of government acquired it. We The People, became government subjects.

Not just the "Rebs," but the entire nation was ruled by the Federal Government, the Constitution becoming what the controlling politicians of the time declared it to be, to be adhered to, or ignored, as political convenience dictated, a condition existing to this day.

This is the authority behind the Judges, Presidents, and Legislators apparent prerogative, for ignoring the Constitution, without regard for their oaths.

Immediately following the war, the mechanism of government was too weak to enforce much of the acquired power, thus the magnitude of change was not recognized at the time, however, the foundation had been laid.

Several abortive attempts to create a national bank, finally culminating in the Federal Reserve, income tax laws, confiscation of constitutional money, and enforcement of prohibition laws, were among the first examples of the expanding power.

However, federal power was not expanded in earnest until the Civil Rights movement. When President Eisenhower justly employed it, for the purpose of enforcing compliance with civil rights laws, the flood gate was opened.

History has again proven that power begets power, and that if it can be misused, it will be misused.

The Constitution, as well as the Bill of Rights, is either ignored, being decimated by the courts, or, as is the case with Second

Amendment, under constant attack.

Our "Damnocratic" government representatives, now unabashedly play the American people like a cheap fiddle, constantly manipulating fact, figures, and information, then "polling" us to determine how much of it we bought.

Remember the statement of the man caught behind the curtain in the Wizard of Oz "don't believe what you see, believe what I tell you!"

Same statement in the form of a question: How many of us will begin to believe our eyes, and how many will continue swallowing the garbage we are being fed?

Because the truth has a nasty habit of playing hell with the spin doctors version of a good story, news correspondents access to events is now determined by whether or not it will benefit government.

"For their protection," at the siege of Waco, none were allowed closer than two miles, while in Iraq they were "embedded" with the troops.

Our politicians, in the name of the federal government--just as the British, in the name of the Monarch--now govern under the cloak of sovereign immunity, sovereignty stolen from We The People.

Under the guise of constant re-interpretation, a facade has been created to disguise and justify this authoritarian government, and sell it to the citizens as Constitutional.

By constant repetition of policy over a period of about fifty years, our "leaders" have replaced a stable Constitutional Republic, with a very unstable, Socialist Damn-ocracy, oblivious to the warning of James Madison that: "Democracies have ever been spectacles of turbulence and contention; have ever been found incompatible with personal security or the rights of property,

and have in general, been as short in their lives as they have been violent in their deaths."

Are these words--a haunting from the grave--a warning which we have chosen to ignore, or do they merely highlight circumstances over which we have had no control, short of another Civil War?

Is it the chosen time for our current cross breed government to face the ultimate judge, the Declaration of Independence?

MY PERSONAL OPINION?

A person must possess their sovereignty before they can voluntarily subjugate a portion of it to a just government. It has taken us over two hundred years, and the most brutal war in our history to achieve the necessary conditions for each and every person, regardless of race, creed, color, and gender, to at least get a fair shot at the brass ring.

The caterpillar is indeed in the process of expiring of old age, that the butterfly may emerge in the form of the true Republic.

Envisioned within the Declaration of Independence, the emergence of the government ordained and managed into existence by the creator of all things; the government impossible to build until now, Is Immanent!

"We hold these truths to be self evident, that all men are created equal, and are endowed by their creator with certain inalienable rights, that among these are life, liberty, and the pursuit of happiness."

With these beliefs and statements, our forefathers justified the killing of "His Majesties" troops, and the overthrow of a government.

If this statement, an affirmation of the dignity and sovereignty of each individual, was an untruth, then our forefathers were

murderers, and our nation was founded illegitimately. (The view of British Royalty for over two centuries.)

If however, the Declaration of Independence is a statement of eternal truth, should every copy be destroyed, the innate principles contained within it, will continue to drive future generations, just as they had driven the many previous generations, prior to Jefferson having committed them to paper.

The document neither builds a government, nor does it mandate a form of government, it merely states the goals of any government to be the securing of individual sovereignty.

"To secure these rights, governments are created among men, deriving their just powers from the consent of the governed."

This uncompromising judge will continue to destroy governments and civilizations until mankind final perceives and acts upon this truth: The essence of the term "the governed" is embodied, in its totality, in each sovereign human being!

In a proclamation consisting of only thirty-six words, Jefferson recognized the intended value of every individual soul, their relationship to each other, and their collective relationship to their creator; the principles comprising the heart and soul of civilization itself.

While the ingenious manner in which the power of government is curtailed and limited by checks and balances, has been hailed as the master piece of representative government, correctly recognizing the source of lawful government to be each individual citizen, was of far greater importance!

Our forefathers, by hypocritically protecting the "right" of slavery, and the denial of universal sovereignty, doomed their government to failure, before it was implemented. Thus the Civil War!

A Constitutional Crisis? What Do You Think?

The selling of indulgences shattered Catholicism, destroying forever the unity of Christianity; that same process, now serving as our "justice system" is producing identical results. When either absolution or justice, becomes a commodity to be bought and sold, you have neither.

Judicially we are rapidly approaching the time that juries will be incapable of rendering important decisions, state governments enact legislation, or the results of elections certified, without the threat of being overturned at some level of the judiciary.

Financially we are tolerating a tax & currency system, even its administrators don't understand.

Politically we have devised no better methods than auction and bribery to choose our leaders; conflict of interest has been expunged from our vocabulary.

Individually we must secure the services of an attorney to either explain the common law of the land, or, have it reinterpreted to our benefit in a court of law.

Morally we are allowing our government representatives to sell our following generations into indentured servitude, to provide present government "services" and future "benefits" that we ourselves are unwilling to pay for.

There is an alternative! The civilization built on the model of the Declaration of Independence, is still in our future!

Self Government is the only viable form of government, all others require libraries of capricious, contradictory law, and an army of (priest) lawyers to interpret and guide the individual through this artificial mine field.

Collective self government must begin with individual self government--but not to worry. If we are indeed beings created in the image and after the likeness of our Creator, along with the inherited sovereignty--derived through education, and the consequences of experience, comes the inherent ability to achieve and maintain that sovereignty.

We have no choice! If the ability exist, so also does the responsibility.

Our Constitution, when applied as the Bill of Rights proves that it was intended, and interpreted according to the Declaration of Independence, is still a very viable contract of government.

The founders of our nation conceived a plan, and laid the cornerstone in the form of our Constitution, for a free citizenry.

Damn-ocracy, (authoritarian government) through debt, has mortgaged our immediate future, as well as that of our following generations, to the International Banking Cartel.

We now find ourselves faced with the task of either capitulating to permanent authoritarian slavery, or dismantling this suffocating financial system with which we have been burdened, and building the envisioned, Free American Republic.

We not only can, but must, redeem our government by electing representatives who value the principles espoused within the Declaration of Independence!

It Is Indeed Time For Another Revolution, But With Ballots, Not Bullets!

A Very Exciting Time And Place To Be Alive!

LINCOLNS QUANDARY

A Shadow Government, Existing Simultaneously With, and Masquerading as, the Legitimate United States Federal Government, Now Exists in the Form of a British Style Corporation.

Whether or not it is formally chartered, it has existed in function since the inception of the Civil War. It is this entity which is in bankruptcy.

Its conception was the result of Lincolns quandary, when faced with the secession of half the states of Union.

In order to preserve the Union, his stated goal; he would be required to convene Congress for the purpose of declaring war on a portion of the states represented. An impossible task!

There were two small problems: It was not unlawful for states who had freely chosen to join the union, to freely choose to withdraw, thus there was neither justification for war, nor entity upon whom the war could be declared.

The very act of declaring war on the Confederacy, would have recognized secession as an accomplished, lawful act, thereby branding the Federal government, a criminal regime.

Should a war prove necessary, he, quite obviously would be faced with the problem of producing an entity on which to both declare and fight a war.

Problem Solved!

After the negotiations between the Federal Government, and the state of South Carolina, over the removal of federal troops, and the return of Fort Sumpter seemingly failed, by attacking the Fort, and forcing the troops to withdraw, the Confederacy had furnished Lincoln his justification, while simultaneous painting themselves as the villain.

While it was lawful to secede, it was not lawful to attack property, either owned, or leased by the Federal Government. Thus the entities making up the Union, the Several States United, and the Federal US, were at war.

The United States government, as originally formed, was too merely serve as an umbrella under which the Several States would unite in common cause, primarily defense, commerce, and common currency.

The District of Columbia and the Federal territories, as designated within the Constitution, were under direct control of Congress and the President, direct power over the states was severely restricted, a sore point, being viewed as a short coming of the Constitution.

Because there was no provision within the Constitution authorizing it, when Lincoln, by Presidential Order, declared nation wide martial law, he set a precedent which is still with us.

Because it was not by act of Congress, it was accomplished by policy, an act of law without foundation, a process which has come to be known as "the color of law."

Initially, preserving the Union by preventing secession of the Southern States was of little importance to the general public, and was generally considered a waste of life and money, thus, persuading men to volunteer for the cause, was not wildly successful.

Lincoln had stated from the outset of the crisis, that if the goal of preserving the union could be accomplished without the freeing the slaves, he would do so. However, after he had been convinced to redefine the war, and clothe it in the noble cause of freedom, recruiting became far more successful.

To this day, the American people are addicted to the word "freedom," just as warriors of other nations were addicted to the rallying cry "For King and Country.

At wars end, the nation was devastated, in mind, body and spirit, and dead broke; however, the British bankers were well aware of its potential, and maintained a concerted effort toward the establishment of a private banking syndicate.

They hit pay dirt in 1913, when under a cloud of impropriety, Congress passed the Federal Reserve Act, thereby handing the keys to the US Treasury, to a consortium of international bankers, headed by the Rothschild family.

The creation of this corporation, instituted within The United States, the same system by which merchant bankers had for centuries, profited from constant hostility and war among the European nations.

It has never been necessary for the banker to initiate the three step Hegelian Principle of: First, creating the problem; Second, pointing it out; Third, offering the prepared solution; government officials for centuries have very successfully employed it.

In like manner, the bankers have, also for centuries, initially financed both antagonist, and then, by withholding funding from their choice of the combatants, determined the victor. As expressed by the Rothschilds: "Control both sides of any conflict, and it matters not who wins or loses, as they will have both been in our debt."

It is no secret that the Rothschilds, with banking houses in Frankfurt, Paris, Vienna, Naples, and London, by supplying funds too various antagonists, gained immensely from political unrest; and they were merely one representative, of the eternal plague.

Add, Hambros, Barings, Warburg, Mattioli, Abs, Lehman Bros.

and the Fuggers, and you have the names of a few more members, of a long list of money manipulators, extending into prehistory, and blanketing the earth.

Until the American revolution, wealth was easy to determine, with much of it transportable. It consisted of precious metals, jewels, spices, works of art, human slaves, and various other artifacts making life "fit for a King" as the saying goes.

The national treasury, belonged to the ruler, and its disbursement was at his, or her pleasure; thus, while chosen "subjects" profited, the lives of the vast majority were dedicated to its enrichment.

The pride of the nation, was embodied by the wealth of the Sovereign, and his/her standard of living. The world was involved in a real-life, continuous chess match, in which the pawns value was determined, merely by its position, in relation to the king.

The conclusion of the Civil War, found the American Citizenry, the conqueror, as well as the conquered, captives of the Corporate Federal Government, the winner was the British Empire.

Six hundred fifty thousand dead Americans; untold wounded and permanently disabled; a nation in ruins; and a bankrupt treasury; one hundred years of "free labor" and hypocrisy, culminating in war, bore a very high price tag, and that was just the beginning!

As with British maritime law, the officers of our new government assumed the sovereign status of the conquered citizenry, and our Constitutional courts of common law, were interspersed with Corporate courts of equity.

While common law prevailed for a number of years, the legal profession eventually overwhelmed much of it.

Thus each individual state, as conquered territory, existed at the pleasure of the Federal Government, the sole occupant of the top rung of the corporate ladder; with the various states comprising the second.

Many versions and variations of corporations now exist, but all share the same basic reality, Corporations Exist at the Pleasure, and under Control of Government.

The fifteen year carpet bagger/reconstruction era was instituted with The Federal US suspending all Constitutional protections, in all of the Corporate States, and allowing the citizens, now corporate property, the degree of freedom deemed appropriate.

Thus, whether in reality or effect, a corporate/shadow version of state government, subservient to the Federal, was created, retaining the prewar procedures and offices, thus perpetuating the illusion of autonomy.

Think Not? Then explain seat belt laws at the instigation of the Federal government, national speed limits, the "right" of the federal government, to determine the validity of Oregon's passed and affirmed, death with dignity law; as well as the validity of California's recall election.

With the incorporation of county, city, and municipal governments, corporate structure has now spread throughout the nation, governing by policy rather than law.

This is reflected by the increasing level of private property being taken by "civil" condemnation laws, in cities and municipalities in virtually every state within the nation, simply for the purpose of increasing tax revenues of a given property, as an example.

Now, acting under the shield of corporate immunity, officers of government at every level, have nothing to lose by utilizing public money for the purpose of instituting, and prosecuting condemnation procedures.

The affected citizens then must use their money, in a fight financed by their money, in the effort toward retaining that which is lawfully theirs!

Damn-ocracy in its natural element!

By practice, and oath, the institutions established by the Constitution were adhered too by their shadows, thus averting the public's awareness of the change.

However, and very importantly, they, by not abolishing it, preserved the original Constitution!

The "Supreme Court" has, in many aspects, adhered to the Constitution, doing an excellent job of establishing equal "rights" of all citizens, per the Declaration of Independence.

However, their status as corporate property was unaltered; they were merely added to the list of fellow citizens, with "rights" defined and permitted at the pleasure of the Federal Government.

Government the facilitator, has thus evolved into government the dictator, throughout the land of the "free," and home of the brave!

The corporate state has slowly evolved into direct democracy, and, as such, is succumbing to the fate predicted by James Madison, "that generally democracies are as violent in their deaths, as they are short in their duration."

Theft, whether perpetrated by an individual or a nation, and either with or without the window dressing known as immanent domain, is still theft.

Unlike a king, Constitutionally, the only thing that the President of the United States possesses, that you or I do not, is temporary title to an office, and the authority to perform the designated functions of the office, to which he/she, by oath agree.

Unlike a crown, no allodial (Constitutional) title exists to any office within the Republic of the United States; nor may any portion of either its commonwealth, or the authority vested in the office, be lawfully transferred.

While Queen Elizabeth 1 possessed the authority to grant a lease on her throne in the form of the corporation, that authority has never been Constitutionally vested, in any office within the United States.

Thus, in 1913, neither the Congress, nor President Wilson, possessed lawful authority to establish the Federal Reserve Corporation, nor did Constitutional authority exist in 1933, when President Roosevelt debased the currency.

It, as well as all other corporations, derive from Presidential Power established by President Lincoln, and successfully enforced by the results of the Civil War.

Money, in its correct perspective, is nothing more than a representation of wealth, and must be backed by collateral, or, as in the case of silver and gold, serve to collateralize itself.

When The Federal Reserve was handed the keys to the treasury, it was stocked with silver and gold, the legitimate backing of our currency. I have heard it said, that as part of the deal, its title was transferred to the syndicate.

Although the citizens money was devalued by about 75%, as the result of Franklin Roosevelt's requiring the citizens to surrender gold for less than eighteen dollars per ounce silver, then, revaluing it to thirty-two dollars per ounce silver, for various reasons, as well as the following, it is likely that the government, at that time, retained title to the gold.

Because gold comprises a major component of our common wealth, it is imperative that its presence be confirmed by a complete audit of the treasury, including all documents, physical count, as well as an assay.

This procedure, although requested, has been refused several times in the past, thus, it will take place, only with a total change of elected representation.

For a number of years, legitimate currency, in the form of silver certificates and Fed notes circulated side by side, and, unless closely examined, were virtually indistinguishable; gold however, remained the standard of account between banks.

Many of us in fact, until Lyndon Johnson, as another symptom of the bankruptcy of 1933 debased our coinage and called in the last of the silver certificates, were barely conscious of the term, federal reserve note.

The process by which our currency came into being, was, and still is a total mystery; the concept of fractional reserve banking we never heard of; and compound interest was a concept we knew had the potential of increasing our savings, if we had anything left from our living expenses.

In short, a government which we have been led to believe all our lives, is of the people, by the people, and for the people, we are discovering to be of, by and for the benefit of the multi-national corporation!

We, The American Citizenry, Between Now And November 2004 , Are Destined To Be Exposed To Everything We Didn't Really Care To Know, About "DAM-OCRATIC" Government!

IN THE IMAGE

"So God Created Man in His Image, in the Image of God Created He Them, Male and Female Created He Them."

By extension, beings created in the Image And After The Likeness of a Sovereign Entity, must themselves be Sovereign.

The mere acknowledgment of this obvious truth, reveals the answer to that most ancient of questions: What Is The Purpose of Life?

That Answer--The only purpose befitting this lofty position is: Dedication to the Goal of Becoming a Species of Self Determining Individuals, Thereby Fulfilling the Mission too Which We Were Created.

Isn't it amazing that it was not necessary to climb mountains, swim oceans, or seek out the remote cave, of the wisest of ancient sages, in order to solve mans most perplexing mystery.

Revealed in the first few words of the worlds most published and widely distributed book, the answer, awaiting acknowledgment, has resided from day one within the heart of every person who has ever pondered the question.

In keeping with this philosophy, it is my conviction that: The moment a dominant portion of mankind finally shakes the dependence upon religious interpretations of God, thereby acknowledging our parentage; accepts our good fortune, thereby recognizing the fact that far more is expected, with far greater rewards, of sons and daughters than is expected of servants; and assumes the attendant responsibilities, The Human Race Will Have Stepped Into an Unobstructed Universe!

This I Have Done; in addition to the rejection of the Christian

contention, that I was conceived in sin, and born of iniquity!

Indebted to neither alter nor throne for my existence, I, a unique Son, individually created in the image and after the likeness of my Creator, am dependant upon neither clergy nor governor, for either salvation or justification!

Therefore, I am not required to fall on my face, get on my knees, contact a priest, nor either join or be added too any religious body, for the purpose of either establishing communication, or enjoying the endowments, <u>inherent of family</u>.

Wherever I find myself, regardless of circumstances, through special entitlement, one of the endowments of my unique status, requires only that I, through thought, open a direct line!

THE AMERICAN PARADOX

Articulated by men, whom, upon discerning this answer-- The Declaration of Independence became the trumpet cry of Our Creator God, announcing the birth of a new paradigm in mankind's development.

Not devised by the mind of Jefferson, but merely revealed, should every copy somehow be destroyed, the innate truths contained within the document will continue to drive mankind's development; providing explanations for previous wars, and justification for future ones, just as before having been committed to paper by his hand.

Thus, we, the citizens of the United States are living in the most paradoxical nation to ever exist.

This condition did not just happen, but was created at the time of birth, indeed, was the purpose of birth of this new nation.

The idea that a government could not only exist, but flourish, to serve the good of the common person, without the existence of an aristocracy, was blasphemous to the prevailing principles of elitism, as well as religion; a poison, which had thoroughly permeated mankind's interpersonal relationships, as well as governments, from our earliest history.

The American Paradox is unique in the fact that, despite the presence of both, we are the first nation to exist within recent history, in which people of all races, creeds and religions, have freely co-existed, and co-operated, under one common language, a major sin if you believe the story of the Tower of Babel found in the bible.

The lack of common communication, thus co-operation, has resulted in constant mistrust and warfare on Planet Earth for thousands of years.

Yet, my impression, as I observe the creation with its amazing cohesion, precision, and conformity to common sense, is of a God of absolute perfection and order; thus it would be an impossibility for beings created In This Image, and After This Likeness, to be created for the purpose of chaos.

Thus, the story too be true, would by necessity be totally out of sync with this observed reality; and the <u>intentional disintegration of a unified race</u>, a very foolish act, of an incredibly foolish God.

Totally Unlikely, As Well As Totally Absurd!

Contrarily, in my opinion, we, the citizens of the United States, have been the privileged participants in a major evolutionary leap in the development of those Created in The Image...; a leap that will eventually result in the <u>Initial Unification of the Species!</u>

Underlying and unobserved factors date back thousands of years, and, if studied correctly, reveal the inherent flaw of religious and governmental philosophies that has precipitated the constant conflict of the worlds populations, giving rise to our current plight.

Our last two generations have done far more than merely espousing the philosophy of fair play, equal rights, justice under the law, and elimination of prejudice. We have created laws attempting to augment all of these changes at various levels of society.

Yet, we still look back fifty years or so, and yearn for the "good old days." The time when there was less strife; when supposedly the attributes of family, honesty, and morality, all combined to create an atmosphere of tranquility, and are dismayed at the turmoil occurring all around us.

Perhaps We Are Expecting Too Much, Too Soon!

A closer look at this Utopian land of the free, white, and twenty-one, epitomized by the TV series "Ozzie and Harriet" "Leave it to Beaver" and "Father Knows Best," reveals a time in which the "nigger" and the woman knew their place, and the white youth didn't question ancient wisdom.

I, a white male, was greatly privileged to have grown through adolescence and into young adulthood during the late 1940's and the entire 1950's.

To have participated in the birth, of what is to be the greatest, and most rapid transformation of the human race; as well as one of the best, and most exciting periods in the history, of not only the United States, but the world, is exiting beyond belief.

I was thereby presented with a brief, interactive preview of the life awaiting the human race, when the day finally arrives that all people are afforded the opportunity of grasping the brass ring of self determination.

Laws create impetus, and are very important, however, it should be abundantly clear that we cannot achieve unity, nor abolish divisiveness, by mandate of law alone.

In keeping with the old adage that: God created time too keep everything from happening all at once, and space too keep it from happening all at the same location, law must be afforded the time and opportunity too change minds and character.

Yet, in the context of human history, the entire existence of the United States spans barely the blink of an eye; and the existence of the "modern" human species, even less, when compared to the existence of the planet.

In the very recent past, many of our churches had succeeded in elevating the practice of hypocrisy to the level of a fine art; preaching the doctrine that their God is no respecter of persons; teaching their children to sing that God loves the little children of all different colors, and yet, for various reasons, including race, denying potential members the privilege of fellowship.

Until very recently, American government at every level, from federal to local, had been created to reflect the age old dictum declaring the natural order of things to be the superiority of the white male. For one third of my sixty-nine years, these statements were the reality of the time.

A few people reading this will make the observation that "my parents or grandparents were not white middle class, they were dirt poor and were able to achieve success by hard work and perseverance, pulling themselves up by their own boot straps."

The truth remains however, generally, a white male face was necessary then, and it certainly does not retard progress, even in today's United States.

The United States is the result of thousands of years of governmental evolution. If we analyze the formation, and the eventual demise, of the many world prominent empires over the last six to ten thousands years, we find merit in each of them. Each left a legacy of achievement, in addition to lessons on the evils of tyrannical authority and misuse of power.

We see death and destruction, degradation, and utter contempt

for mankind. However, we also see the wise use of personal power; of love shown to their fellow human beings; a sense of responsibility too, and sorrow over the adversity to befall their "subjects."

While it is clear to us in retrospect, that no person is endowed by God to rule another, to own another, nor to take the life and property of another, this nation was the first ever founded to recognize and challenge this fallacy.

*** Before anyone gets all excited about this statement, reminding me that Great Britain abolished slavery before the United States, just remember, anyone who is the subject of a "Sovereign" King or Queen, by definition, is property of their domain.**

This fallacy, although not condoned by our creator, was allowed to occur that evolution, the chosen means of advancing the species, could complete the transformation of an infant, into a self determining giant.

Interference at any stage of the process, would rob the child created In The Image..., from achieving the self determining status, to which it was created.

I realize that this statement will not set well with many church people, who have been taught that man fell from the grace of God, and as punishment, was denied the status to which we were created.

Obviously, had I agreed with this doctrine, I would not have wasted my time writing what amounts to a rebuttal.

Do I have a hatred of religion? No! I was raised in a religious atmosphere, have a very good foundation in the tenets of Christianity, and have many fond memories of my church affiliations.

We should all be free to communicate with, obey, and conform to, our unique version of the Supreme Being.

I reiterate: "I Am Unique!" "Well So Are You!"

When enough of us recognize our parentage, and respond accordingly, human intellect will soar, and those Created in the Image.... will bask in peace and prosperity.

This evolutionary process is now occurring so rapidly, that we literally wake to a new reality every morning.

My participation in this extravaganza; observing age old "truth" daily being disproved, resulted in my graduation from Christian, to Deist Perception.

A glimpse into our past through my Deist eyes, reveals a guiding, not a controlling hand, thus I foresee neither "Salvation, "Armageddon, nor hell and damnation in our future; I do see, as in our past, serious repercussions from actions which we ourselves are permitted to originate.

While I am open to common sense discussion, I no longer waste time debating doctrine; nor do I attempt to transform anyone's beliefs to that of my own. I simply state my opinion, and am not concerned with how it is received.

I do object to laws which force me to live in conformance with any religious doctrine, doctrine daily growing less relevant, while revealing the fact that: Priest hoods, Not God, Created Prohibitions on Knowledge.

Although in direct contradiction too, and thus prohibited by, that espoused by very powerful and jealous priesthood's, information, innovations, and advancement, were introduced by individuals imbued with special knowledge, and understanding.

Although the messengers were often killed, tortured, imprisoned, or banished, and attempts made to destroy the knowledge; it was seemingly protected, took root, and flourished, thus advancing the infant species.

A surprising number of these special individuals, motivated by the principle of self determination, were somehow concentrated in a very small area on the North American Continent.

A document destined to change the world was written, a new nation born, and in a period of less than two hundred years, less than ten percent of the worlds population, was entrusted with more power, and guidance in it use, than the other ninety percent combined.

An accident? Not likely! To my way of thinking it was the nurturing hand of the Creator, placing the feet of those Created in the Image.. on the correct path.

The United States, a key part of the plan, has been the class room in which this principle has been taught, and its disciples have spread to every corner of the globe.

The complete truth embodied in the statement has not been fully implemented, even in this nation, yet no one can deny the impact on the entirety of mankind which even this limited application has produced.

As an example: The advances in interpersonal relationships within my lifetime are difficult to believe.

My life has spanned very nearly one third that of the nation.

I was born less than seventy years after the conclusion of our most devastating war; a war amongst ourselves.

We were still a very divided people; the black race was still in bondage; the women of the nation, in many respects still subservient to men, had gained the right to vote less than fifteen years previously; and we were only seven years away from another war which would engulf the globe, claiming millions more lives, many of them American.

Yet, in the nearly seventy years which I have enjoyed upon this earth, those Created in The Image... have made advances, a study of history reveals should have required centuries.

How Was This Possible?

Well in my opinion, again in contrast to the Christian religion, secrets have never existed between the created and the creator, only mysteries.

While secrets must be revealed, mysteries may be solved through investigation, and the acquisition of knowledge. You know, the "sin," that according too religious teaching, robbed man of eternal life, while evoking the eternal Roth of God, upon the female sex.

In truth, the Eternal Relegation of the Created Image, to the role of mere gardeners, thus denying us the experiences of exploration, discovery, recognition and development of the intuitive cognizance, of our unlimited potential, would have amounted to Eternal Condemnation, to the Hell of Eternal Frustration.

My Acceptance of This Trait, in The Character of My God, Is Not Possible!

In this context, not only was ignorance never intended for the Created Image, but denial of knowledge was an impossibility.

This supposition is borne out by the fact that the knowledge of molecular structure, atomic structure, and genetics, the basic engineering of our physical body, was always at our disposal, too be unveiled over time, by the implementation of the intellect, inherent of design.

If we examine the mechanical format of our electronic computer, we discover two basic elements around which the system is constructed, Random Access Memory (working

memory) and Disk Drive. (stored memory)

Where did this format come from? In my opinion, again, it was an intuitive copy of the original format of those created In The Image...

Because the human body was created from the dust of the earth and was never intended to live forever, contrary to what many of the bible "interpreters" assert, that which was created In The Image... was not so much a creation, as the manifestation of eternal spirit.

Each and every human brain, regardless of nationality or gender, is a personal computer, hooked to the mainframe of the universal mind of our creator.

The human body, fashioned to serve as the earthly transportation vehicle, was designed to assist the spirit in the completion of that portion of the mission, to which it was committed, a process for the replication of replacements bodies was designed into it.

The brain of each human body serves the role of immediate, or working memory.

Nothing is Lost!

The information thus collected, in its totality, forever accumulates within the universal mind, and, benefiting from the consequences, mankind determines the advantages of right versus wrong, and true versus false, culminating with the evolutionary advancement, of the entire species.

By recognizing the scope of a problem, seeking answers to questions from the varied experiences of our brothers and sisters, and with a little assistance from the creator, that which was seemingly insurmountable, will vanish.

Am I Wrong? Perhaps!

However, the various versions of just the Christian religion, devised from unique interpretations of the common foundation, offers very solid testimony to the fact that I will not be the first.

The technological advances within my life time, though having improved the living conditions of a majority of the earths population, are difficult to believe.

Having witnessed, and benefited from their development, too realize that they are merely the necessary first steps to unimaginable progress, although difficult to fathom, is exciting beyond belief.

They have demonstrated to the entire population, the fact that mankind can be the master of our own destiny, and has set the stage for the demise of "dinosaur government;" government structure which dates into pre-history, a way of thinking, which, with periodic updating, has continuously plagued mankind.

Viewing the occurrences in world history and the United States influence in shaping these events, I believe that it is now possible to answer the question posed to the Great Spirit over one hundred and fifty years ago, by a very wise American.

A member and leader of The Suquamish people, an Indian tribe of the Pacific Northwest, Chief Sealth, in a speech delivered in 1851 in response to an offer by the Federal Government to buy land owned by his people, will make any thinking person, seriously question just who was the savage. I somehow do not believe that Chief Sealth would mind my excerpting a portion of his wisdom.

I quote: "This we know; the earth does not belong to man; man belongs to the earth. All things are connected. We may be brothers after all. We shall see.

One thing we know which the white man may one day discover; our God is the same God.

You may think now that you own Him, as you wish to own our land, but you cannot. He is the God of Man, and his compassion is equal for the red man, and the white.

This earth is precious to Him, and to harm the earth is to heap contempt on its creator. The whites too shall pass, perhaps sooner than all other tribes.

Contaminate your bed and you will one night suffocate in your own waste. But in your perishing, you will shine brightly, fired by the strength of the God who brought you to this land, and for some special purpose, gave you dominion over this land, and over the red man.

That destiny is a mystery to us, for we do not understand, when the buffalo are all slaughtered, the wild horses are tame, the secret corners of the forest heavy with the scent of many men, and the view of the ripe hills blotted by talking wires, where is the thicket? Gone. The end of living, and the beginning of survival." close quote

You were right Chief Sealth, we are indeed brothers, and not only the red and white, but all races.

The white race will indeed vanish, but only symbolically, as we recognize the equality demonstrated within this former land of the Red Man.

The life style of the Red Man was sacrificed, in order that the technology then being born, and the attendant changes, could benefit all mankind.

It is only now becoming possible to comprehend the mystery which you did not understand, and even now, over one hundred fifty years later, few people are cognizant of that answer.

Your Beloved Land, Became the Cradle of the Brotherhood of Man!

The foundation has been laid for a new age, in which it will be possible for all the inhabitants of the earth, to not only survive but prosper.

We have made many mistakes, but we have also demonstrated that the majority of people, regardless of race, if given the opportunity, prefer peace to war; and compassion, love and kindness are not the exception, but the rule of every race.

We have a long way to go as we begin the process of cleaning up the attendant mess the new technology has created, but we have an eternity in which to accomplish it.

The world, as a place to live, has definitely benefited as a result of the birth of the United States.

As night falls upon the old power structures, very shortly, all mankind can look with great anticipation, to the bright beautiful dawning, of the morning of the new day.

It is indeed interesting, that a so called savage, should have such an inspirational conception of a Creator God, recognizing and accepting the directing hand of God, appreciating the mighty works of God, and the relationship existing between all creation.

Is it any wonder that the claim of Christianity, to the only religious truth, and their self appointed role as keepers of the gate to salvation, is considered extremely presumptuous by many people?

The honor of being considered you brother Chief Sealth, would be all mine!

Many varied philosophies of life and religion have intermingled to blend the diverse races. As they have interacted, intermarried and learned to work together, an evolutionary process has occurred, at a very accelerated pace.

The new nation became a laboratory, as well as a potential battle ground, in which every possible facet of interpersonal relationships must be confronted.

In this nation, it has been conclusively proven that no race holds a monopoly on love, hate, compassion, caring, hope, dreams, and especially intelligence.

Indeed the children of the Korean and Vietnamese people whom we were characterizing as "mere gooks" a short time ago, are now embarrassing many of the children of our white race, on common intelligence tests.

A microcosm of a diverse world, and the culmination of an evolutionary cycle thousands of years in the making, the United States was created for the express purpose of rectifying circumstances responsible for the reprehensible conditions, which had been the constant scourge of mankind.

A New Man For A New Age!

The intended consequences of this giant forward leap in mankind's evolution has not been a disappointment.

The new way of thinking, sans the means of implementation, made no sense, consequently, it is no accident that the location of the nursery was very sparsely populated, geographically remote, and furnished with any and all items required for total self reliance, thus, that which could be conceived, could also be accomplished.

Semi-isolation from conditions which had existed for thousands of years, afforded the opportunity to re-evaluate the old, and obviously flawed perspective of life.

The opportunity to formulate and institute a new course, for not only the new nation, but for a new world, yielded immediate results.

Individual initiative toward innovation, resourcefulness, and implementation of new discoveries, attributes which had, too a great extent lain dormant or suppressed, suddenly flowered; and what a flowering!

Although the full magnificence of this garden is far from having been achieved, the record of accomplishments derived from even the limited discovery, and implementation of our created potential is astounding.

Although this virtual isolation existed for over a hundred years, there was never a dull moment. The pioneers brought more problems with them than they were able to resolve, not the least of which was elitism. But we have made exceptional progress.

As I consider the tidal wave of change now sweeping the globe, rather than cower in fear and trepidation, I am thanking my creator for not only the privilege of being a participant in this epic event, but for the blessings of its recognition.

The simple recognition of individual self determination, as the coveted" Brass Ring" sought by every preceding generation, and for which every future generation is destined to strive, constitutes innate wisdom; a truth which rings in timeless harmony, with each individual soul.

Individual Sovereignty The Principle, Individual Freedom The Reality!

THE SANCTITY OF LIFE

Inherent sanctity of created life, now where do you suppose I acquired that quaint idea?

Or the equally absurd notion, that governments are not endowed with the authority to arbitrarily determine one individual, or even nations of individuals, lives to be acceptable sacrifices, in order to accomplish certain political goals?

Perhaps in the writing of some long forgotten scholar? Oh, now I remember! A little over two hundred years ago, a man named Jefferson, penned a document which he entitled, The Declaration of Independence in which he espoused these ideas as fact.

This document was then presented to a king by a small group of people, claiming the right to form a government founded upon this novel idea.

Treasonous, thundered the kings of the earth, and blasphemous echoed the priest hoods!

How could mere commoners be so presumptuous as to assert that with his/her first breath, an individual not only claimed his/her life, but an endowment of sovereignty.

A nation of sovereign individuals? Preposterous!

No one possess the right to live without a king, and certainly not the freedom to choose their own religion, or, heaven forbid, choose to live without it.

With Priestly sanctification, of Kingly denunciations, war was declared upon the criminal upstarts.

SANCTITY OF LIFE

Although a distant three thousand miles and no threat to his empire, the King still considered it a major threat to his national interest.

The Heathens Must Be Disarmed, he again thundered!

Thus, a flotilla of ships laden with troops and the latest military equipment, was immediately dispatched, and the battle was joined.

After the smoke cleared however, the heathens had won the right to create their government.

Although unrecognizable today, a government, founded supposedly upon the premise of inherent sanctify of created life, and individual sovereignty, did indeed come into being.

I find it very fascinating, that over two hundreds years before the fact, our third president revealed the absurdity of the thought process of the forty-third, with a proclamation consisting of merely fifty-six words.

"We hold these truths to be self evident, that all men are created equal; that they are endowed with certain unalienable rights; that among these are, life, liberty and the pursuit of happiness. That to secure these rights, governments are created among men, deriving their just powers from the consent of the governed."

A proclamation in which he recognized the intended value of every individual soul, their relationship to each other, and their collective relationship to their creator; the heart and soul of civilization itself.

Something To Consider

Abundant resources, a profusion of fresh water, rich farm land, beauty beyond compare, temperature conducive to life, and a dominate species possessing unbridled intelligence; an

amalgamation which can and should produce peace, tranquility and a world peopled with happiness.

We find instead, thousands of years of constant warfare; weapons systems improved from rocks to thermonuclear bombs, and the current population seriously flirting with the ultimate disaster.

What the hell is wrong with the human race?

Summed up in eight words the answer is: greed, politics, arrogance, and utter lack of civilization!

For six thousand years, improvements in death dealing technologies, including communications, have been in the vanguard of our scientific advances.

Now, courtesy of this communications technology, millions of people can be whipped into a fighting frenzy by two men preening like peacocks before television cameras; one brandishing a shotgun, the other hydrogen bombs.

They, and their families, ringed and protected by soldiers and body guards with weapons at the ready; were preparing for war, neither of which really gives a damn how many people die, or who they are, so long as they are inhabitants of another country.

My How Things Change

Our "Christian nation" has now been successfully "educated" to accept and approve anything which those in authority choose to feed us.

Under the first Bush Presidency, we watched transfixed, and judging by our silence, with approval, as innocent people, by the tens of thousands, became the "acceptable sacrifice " to get one man, the same man for whom, under a following Bush Presidency, many other lives were to be sacrificed.

Demeaned as collateral damage, the lives of men, women and children who just happened to be occupying buildings targeted by "smart bombs" were accorded the same value as the building.

How and why have our values changed so dramatically in less than one generation?

Only a few years ago a young lieutenant named Calley was tried, found guilty and sentenced to twenty years in prison for ordering troops under his command, to shoot innocent civilians in Vietnam.

Although following military protocol of the time, protocol derived from some very unpleasant past experiences, the American people, the military, and the President were outraged that a man that Congress had commissioned an "officer and gentleman" was capable of so dastardly an act.

Although Federal Law requires that eighty percent of the original sentence be served before an individual is even eligible for parole, quite likely as a reward for keeping his mouth shut, and not embarrassing superiors much higher in the chain of command, Lieutenant Calley served only a few months.

As things are now playing out, regardless of how much time he served, it was a miscarriage of justice.

This observation, invites an interesting question or three: Just how do those in "authority" determine the criteria under which selected innocent individuals qualify as "collateral" damage," while others "enjoy" the dubious honor of being classified as murder victims?

How does the use of bombs rather than bullets alter this equation?

Which is an act of terrorism? A bomb blows a 747 out of the sky,

another destroys a building in Baghdad?

Does it really matter whether a bomb carried by the airplane explodes among innocent people in the sky, or is dropped to explode among innocent people on the ground, except in the perspective of those involved?

Our nation bombed the hell out of downtown Baghdad for days, collapsing buildings and killing untold numbers of innocent men, women and children.

Why then should it come as a shock, that the citizens of Baghdad would rejoice when airplanes bring down buildings within one of our major cities; damage the nerve center of a military establishment responsible for those bombings, and the resultant "collateral damage"?

Are you offended when the loss of over three thousand innocent American lives is dismissed as acceptable, as the term "collateral damage" implies?

Ask yourself just why the terms do not seem to equate when the collapsed buildings are in the heart of our nation, and the innocent lives are American family members?

Just how do we acquire credence while extolling our vaunted value of human life, while denouncing citizens of other nations as lacking in these virtues, when our values stop at our nations borders?

By labeling Iraqi citizens as acceptable collateral damage, do we not so label ourselves? Consider the events of September 11, 2001 before you answer.

What is our justification for a preemptive attack? Am I free to kill my neighbors family because I suspect that he possess the means of doing me harm, but will not allow me to search his home to find proof?

Remembering Waco Texas, and Ruby Ridge Idaho isn't this the same "rational" position not only endorsed, but acted upon, by the gun control zealots within our own government, and against our fellow citizens?

Collateral damage, or murder?

Given the fact, that thanks to a sympathetic press and an indifferent religious community, the Damn-ocratic President, was not only held blameless, but was re-elected.

A very good indicator, that the American people are comfortable with the current "acceptable sacrifice" concept, even when those sacrifices are innocent fellow citizens!

The natural conclusion then is: that the concept of murder doesn't exist, if it is the by-product of Damnocratic law enforcement!

What happened to the loudly proclaimed American virtue, of respect for the value of created life?

We are not innocents when we allow our leaders to start a war. Not one citizen faced danger in our country, for attempting to prevent it.

This was not so of our fellow human beings in Baghdad.

They were, and are, in a no win situation. Unable to stop the war, and unable to stop the current reprisals. From either direction, they are dead if they try, or dead if they don't.

How does merely classifying them collateral damage (acceptable sacrifices), justify our killing innocent Iraqi citizens with explosives, while demonizing Hussien for utilizing gas to achieve the same result?

We can support our President, and cheer the death of the "godless Muslims," but the exact degree of barbarity we are

willing to extend in our dealings with the "enemy" we can expect in return.

While we were in the position to declare war, the assumption that we would be in the position of declaring peace, was totally absurd.

By what right can we expect our lives to be accorded anymore respect, and consideration, than that which we display toward the lives of our "enemy".

Just remember, any rules of war which we establish are in effect from now on. If bombs are set on our planes, and disease and chemicals unleashed in our cities, any protest which we make will echo with the dull thud of hypocrisy.

Every major city, in every nation has military advantage, and as such, according to criteria established by our own leaders, satisfies the requirement, and justifies any and all collateral damage incurred in the wake of an attack.

By preemptively attacking the capital city of a nation, and inflicting terrible damage and death, we have marked every city, and every citizen on earth, as acceptable targets.

Previously, by throwing Lieutenant Calley to the wolves, our government was able to extricate the United States from the sewer of world opinion.

By characterizing him as a low ranking criminal, not indicative of true leadership, our military command and civilian government was able to "white wash" the incident.

Now however, accounts televised around the world of President Bush 1, with approval of the United Nations, justifying this "collateral damage" before the fact, responsibility for the barbarity has been expanded to include every collaborative nation.

By supporting this action we, collectively, have destroyed any distinction between soldier and civilian, and have painted an even larger target on our own backs.

The attack in Spain proves the point!

If we can expect the same level of government "protection" from the importation of Anthrax that we receive from drugs and aliens, it would seem that the last thing we need to be doing is cultivating enemies by the hundreds of millions.

For years our leadership has painted Saddam Hussein as an unprincipled criminal; a megalomaniac, who has managed, through utter ruthlessness, to acquire, and, even resorting to the use of poison gas against his own people, to maintain dictatorial control of a strategically important nation.

It's all true! Saddam supplied both the paint and the brush!

However, the same can be said of many other regimes around the world, regimes which are supported by our government, our armed might, our tax dollars, and, as with Iraq, our trade dollars.

Whether or not the man possessed weapons of mass destruction was of little importance, because we know for a fact, that while he did possess the delivery system capable of threatening Israel, the same is not true as it relates to the United States.

It is also abundantly clear that, thanks to the United States, Israel is entirely capable of taking care of herself, not only with conventional weapons, but, again thanks to the United States, with weapons of mass destruction.

We also know for a fact, that compared to Russia, which possessed both weapons and delivery systems, and which we did manage to contain, Iraq would have been simplicity itself. A fact we proved for ten years!

China and North Korea at this time, offer a far greater threat to our welfare than did Iraq. Because they now possess both the weapons as well as the delivery system, the goal of world peace would much farther advanced by their disarmament.

So why was President Bush so obsessed with the conquering of Iraq, as opposed to North Korea?

The answer, as evidenced by current conditions, appears obvious, although contradictory to the managed information spoon fed the American populace by our governmental authorities.

As the political climate of Saudi Arabia daily becomes more precarious, it is quite obvious that the United States was in desperate need of a more secure presence within the Arabian oil patch.

The Bush administration, by blowing the weapons issue totally out of proportion, convinced themselves that they had created a smoke screen, capable of cloaking the necessity of a military presence within the Middle-east, secured by a more durable arrangement than "invitation."

However, the truth of the strategic importance to the United States of Iraqi oil reserves, is much to large to be obscured by so thin a screen.

In short, when President Bush rolled the dice, he was absolutely positive that it was a sure thing.

Failure to immediately establish his justification was an embarrassment; failure to establish it at all, has become his worse nightmare. And his declaration that we "know" manifested, in the vernacular of the Apache Indians--as speaking with a forked tongue, visible to the entire world.

While our government is ranting and raving about the lack of all

out commitment of European governments to our point of view; a perceived betrayal of a debt owed the US, by our intervention on their behalf in World War 11, we are overlooking the first hand experience of war fought in their cities, and in their homes.

Man kind has transitioned from one man fighting another with bare hands, through wars fought with clubs, knives, explosives and even nuclear bombs.

Weapons have now become so powerful, so small, and so deadly, that one person can now destroy or render entire cities uninhabitable, the trigger nothing more than hopelessness or religious fanaticism.

Must we explore the utter depravity of man, or isn't it time that we attempt to reverse this cycle of hate and violence?

Why wait until the earth is scorched with nuclear fire, ravaged with man induced disease, and our air and water poisoned by chemicals?

If not now when, if not us who?

Have we learned nothing from Israel's futile attempt to create an impenetrable fortress, as a shield from hate?

In their elitism, they have succeeded in marking Tel Aviv, as the most desirable, as well as the most vulnerable target on earth; a setting duck, awaiting the inevitable.

Someone must display the courage to attempt to derail this circus of horrors; a six thousand year run is long enough; and the US is the only nation with resources, credibility, and leadership, with which to even attempt to accomplish the task!

America, it is time to begin constructing the civilization of individual sovereignty, in accordance with the principles espoused within our own Declaration of Independence!

EVILS OF GOVERNMENT

Was Justice Served by Government Action in Waco?

If not, then a crime was committed, and just as in Oklahoma City, both events carried a death sentence for many innocent people, including children.

President Clinton, as well as most citizens, recognized the fact that the severity of the alleged crimes, did not warrant the magnitude of the action.

Twenty years previously, a president had been driven from office as the result of a burglary of which he had no fore knowledge. In so short a time, had our national sense of justice deteriorated to the point, that any steward could reasonably conclude the use of automatic weapons, as well as gas against children and citizens not even charged with a crime, to be consistent with his or her duties?

At the very least the Congressional hearing into the Waco tragedy should have supplied answers to this question, as well as the following ones: Is a search warrant in the hands of Federal officers tantamount to an enhanced right to kill?

Do Federal police officers enjoy the right to consider the death of innocent people an acceptable price to serve a search warrant?

Because the focus of the investigation became errors made in the conduct of the raid, rather than its legitimacy, these issues were not even addressed.

By default then, in the minds of those individuals in control of the awesome power of government, the answer to the question is YES, which, in itself, poses another question: From whence do these enhanced rights derive?

Until this question is addressed, our nation will careen from one disaster to another.

In a system of government consisting solely of sovereign individuals, by definition the only legitimate existing source of rights is that possessed by each individual.

Interestingly enough, no individual citizen may conclude that because an event is possible, that it will occur.

While we may each arm ourselves for the purposes of self defense, the act of preemptively attacking another whom we suspect harbors the intent, and whom we suspect possess the means to harm us, is considered and is prosecuted as assault.

The same must hold true for law enforcement officers!

According to the Declaration of Independence, our government officials operate by the consent of the governed, under a delegation of authority, not surrendered rights.

Thus in the minds of many very scared, angry, and well armed citizens, the answer to the original question is a very emphatic NO.

These officials not only do not enjoy the enhanced right to kill, but, because the citizens do not possess the right themselves, there no basis upon which authority may even be delegated.

Thus, like two trains, screaming toward each other on the same track, the stage is set for one hell of a collision.

Personal responsibility, and respect for life and property, was drilled into me in a police academy in the early 60's.

I was taught that the purpose of the weapons with which I was entrusted was for my personal protection, in situations instigated by others, not to enforce the law.

Our mission was to prevent, if possible, not intentionally instigate situations in which the use of these weapons was required.

In the space of forty years, has the need for the qualities of responsibility, respect, and common sense become antiquated, or, has their demise merely become an unfortunate casualty in our exuberance toward law enforcement at the police, rather than the court level?

The amount of evil in government, is determined by that which we tolerate.

How much responsibility and respect for the lives of innocent fellow Americans, was displayed by President Clinton and Janet Reno during the continuing atrocity in Waco Texas, including the gassing of children, when either possessed the authority to halt the slaughter at any time?

How much responsibility, displayed in all its glory for fifty-one days on world wide television, was exercised by those entrusted with weapons ranging from automatic rifles, to tanks and helicopters?

How much respect was shown for innocent life, when officers, recognizing the danger, instigated a life and death situation, only after protecting themselves with body armor?

How many churches publicly deplored and criticized the government attack?

How many newspaper and television editorials demanded an end to the siege?

We all are very cognizant of the fact that the answer to all the questions was: VIRTUALLY NONE!

In addition, a very large percentage of "we the people "accepted the Congressional investigative farce, perpetrated in the name of justice, without criticism?

Why then was it not surprising that in our "Damn-ocracy" President Clinton's approval rating did not suffer over a few lies, manipulation of facts, and reinterpretation of the language, a few years later?

Waco, Texas or Oklahoma City, Oklahoma, the philosophy was identical in both instances.

The officials representing the government at Waco, considered the death of innocents, an acceptable price to "get" one man; the bomber at Oklahoma City considered the death of innocents to "get" a few of the participants in the Waco atrocity acceptable, the ends justified the means in both instances.

Both events were criminal acts, yet while the bomber paid the ultimate price for the destruction at Oklahoma City, not one member of the "Damn-ocracy" was even charged in the conflagration at Waco.

The failure of any organization, from the family to the government, begins with its foundation .

Are we really incapable of recognizing the link between our defunct criminal justice system, and our obsession with the "right" to know, trial by press, and guilt by accusation and association?

David Koresh was accused by government of criminal conduct, and the press was only too happy to try, convict and condemn him, and, by silence, approve the execution of all those linked too him by association, after the fact.

How about the link between our educational crisis, and our compulsion for entertainment that insults the intelligence of a normal 12 year old child?

How can we expect our teachers to overcome this defacto school of barbarity, violence, vulgarity, fraud, deceit, greed and sexual irresponsibility?

Individual and societal self determination are now irrevocably intertwined, neither is possible without the other, and neither is possible without the proper government.

Our nations founders laid the cornerstone for this government, a government in which every citizen was both governor and governed; their progeny (us) were to be the builders.

With the Second Amendment they literally put a gun to our collective heads; by retaining the means of individual dissent, they mandated justice as the price of peace.

The truth is, there is no free ride; as with physics, for every action there is an equal and opposite reaction; a penalty is attendant with every crime. If the price is not demanded of the perpetrator, then by default it transfers to the whole of society.

The American people were required to absorb the consequences of Waco, rather than requiring it of the participants, Oklahoma City suffered those consequences.

Each of us, without exception, must be made aware of the fact, that by our actions, we sentence ourselves to the consequences of failure to obey just law, this constitutes the ultimate fulfillment of the process of self determination.

Various judges actively seek "reasons" to exempt the criminal; others "interpret" the Constitution to compromise the Bill of Rights; a President issues "pardons" for no other reason than political expediency; in either instance, the guilty individual or group escapes the full consequences of his action; society picks up the tab; and the law abiding citizens loses another portion of our individual sovereignty.

WAS JUSTICE SERVED

Under any circumstance, the President owed the American people an accounting of his decisions.

However, as we are all aware, while Janet Reno had the balls to accept responsibility, Clinton did not; choosing instead to hide behind "her" trousers!

If the Republicans desire was to remove Bill Clinton from office by way of impeachment, why wasn't he and Janet Reno both subjected to not only that, but prison as well?

Why should the Republican effort to impeach the President over comparative trivialities meet with favor, when their silence was deafening when confronted with these easily provable, impeachable offenses?

Are we really too blind to the relationship between cause and effect, that we can't recognize the links?

Apparently so!

God have mercy, we can't afford justice.

NATIONAL RIFLE ASSOCIATION

" God Created Men, But Samuel Colt Made Them Equal."

This statement is as true today, as it was when originally uttered over one hundred years ago.

Brute strength was rendered obsolete, when the ability to stop the largest animal, or the most murderous human being, was encased within a small metal cylinder.

Now a frail woman, or an infirm man must no longer be dependent upon a champion for his or her defense; any attempt at denying them this protection, rises to the level of criminal conduct.

In addition, the invention of gun powder, and the refinement of the weapons employing this new technology, marked the beginning of the end of tyrannical control of the worlds population.

Until that time, the statement that: "all just power of government derives from the consent of the governed," as postulated within the Declaration of Independence, was nothing but an impossible dream.

The perpetuation of the fulfillment of this dream, and the tribute to the men and weapons responsible for the accomplishment of the miracle, was, and is, the driving force of the National Rifle Association.

The familiarization and skill with firearms, and the continued training, courtesy of the NRA, gave our nation a running start when time was of the essence, and our freedom was at stake; an organization deserving of nothing but platitude.

Thus, the insinuations of the news media, that the National Rifle

Association is responsible for the crime, violence, and drug problems prevalent within the nation, strikes large numbers of admirers, as not only despicable, but slanderous.

However, for many of us, the fact that so many of our fellow citizens fail to either recognize, or, acknowledge, the blatantly hypocritical posture, is even more disturbing.

The record of no other organization within the United States, displays more responsibility to the American way of life, than does that of the National Rifle Association.

It is indeed interesting, that within the over one hundred year history of the organization, they have only recently come under attack by the news media.

What is so surprising is the offense: The CRIME of insisting that the Supreme law of the land be adhered to, and that the elected officials honor their oath to protect and defend that Constitution.

While they take offense at the National Rifle Associations refusal to compromise their stance, they themselves are on a relentless crusade to persuade various "influential" members of the government to perjure their oaths.

Restrictions have been placed upon this technology; denied the common citizen; and enforced under the penalty of death, in virtually every nation, including the United States; conditions much of the news media are attempting to reinstate--permanently

Yet, though we have been criticized, even by our own press, as the only "advanced" nation in which citizens may freely own and carry weapons, while other nations were creating border guards to keep their citizens from leaving, we have had to post guards to control those attempting to get in.

While other "advanced" nations fear that weapons in private hands will we used to overthrow the government, most of our thinking citizenry realize that because of these weapons, any attempt to forcibly seize power, would be an act of suicide.

The reasons for these restrictions then is quite obvious: to control and maintain ownership of the individual citizen, and to prevent an attempt to replace those in control of the government.

This fact is proven within our own nation, merely be remembering the "crime" of either selling, or furnishing, firearms to the Indian population, and the death sentence for a slave to be caught with a weapon.

Although the freedom to enjoy life, without the necessity of personally defending this freedom, is now taken for granted by many of our citizens, this concept is of recent vintage.

Our forefathers were well aware of the inherent dangers of investing total trust in armed organizations, to always act in the best interest of individual freedom.

They knew better than to voluntarily divest themselves of the means to insure that the power inherent within this trust, was not usurped and institutionalized.

They understood the act of willfully surrendering the right and means of personal protection to be asinine.

They knew the name of a nation in which the police and soldiers are armed, and the citizens are not, to be a police, or military state.

They Knew These Things, Because They Were The Conditions From Which They Were Willing to Pledge Their Live, Fortunes, and Sacred Honor to Escape!

In a Republic, the Ultimate Minority, Is the Minority of One, Each Individual Citizen, As Is The Ultimate Majority!

Because each individual is endowed with total natural rights, regardless of the number of members any organization, including government, boasts, the accrued rights, still total only that of one individual, but then how can you improve upon total?

Thus, when accusations are made against an organization, the attack is directed toward each individual within the group.

The Constitution is, among other things, a contract between the citizens, and the people elected to fill the offices created by this contract.

Is it not an established legal principal, that if a contract is broken by either party, then that contract is null and void?

Does our Constitution not contain specific language concerning the right to keep and bear arms?

Is this not also a direct acknowledgment of the right of self defense?

Who would you say would be on the more solid ground, the National Rifle Association, for insisting that the elected officials honor their oath of office, by living up to the conditions of the oath, or, the news media, for insisting that the elected officials perjure that oath, by creating laws in direct contradiction, to the Supreme Law of the land?

Although by intent, sparingly employed, the men who authored the Constitution incorporated the means of its alteration within the document itself, and the states ratified this clause.

Disregarding the parts which caused trouble in resolving immediate problems, the current method endorsed and advocated by the news media, was not that means.

If violence occurs as the government attempts to enforce these laws, who would you say is at fault?

A criminal has been created; is it the law abiding citizen, found not to be trusted, not by the courts, but by the legislature without trial, or, is it the politicians who broke the contract, thereby destroying the base of lawful government?

What is the news media's responsibilities for any loss of life or civil disobedience, occurring as the result of their advocating the disregarding of the Supreme Law?

Are they not accessories to the act?

By Contrast, the National Rifle Association Has Never in its History, Even Remotely Suggested That Any Law Be Disregarded.

How can any media personality justify the character assassination now taking place, without one scrap of evidence in their favor?

The men and women making up this organization run the gamut of a cross section of American life.

They are the teachers who teach your children, the doctors who tend your illnesses, the policeman and firemen who protect your well being and the merchant from which you buy your food, clothing and transportation. They are the clergyman, the plumber, the journalist, and yes, even the television executive.

I personally in the past have been both a soldier, policeman, and member of the National Rifle Association.

To castigate either, or any, of the people comprising any, or all, of these groups, by assassinating the reputation of the organization, is to dishonor millions of honorable men and women.

Men and women who have died for the purpose of achieving, and maintaining, that very fragile treasure, we call freedom.

Once the contract is routinely broken, how long do you think it will be after my gun is confiscated, until your typewriter is stilled, and your television camera controlled?

Can we have one without the other? History, and current events says, NO.

There is a constant refrain concerning the right of free press; I would appreciate someone explaining to me the difference between using the right to keep and bear arms to deny the nation the right of free press, or, of using the right of free press to deprive the nation of the right to individual self defense.

To seek to destroy one freedom by the use of another is stupid enough but it doesn't end there, it cuts the very heart out of the criminal justice system.

Most private citizens, members of the press, and officials of government, consider it repugnant to try a person for a crime, simply because they were either in close proximity to, or, have had contact with, a known criminal.

Why then do many of them seem to have no trouble justifying the casting of an inanimate object, in the form of a gun, as a criminal, and then, trying law abiding citizens for the crime of guilt by association.

Under these circumstances, the charge itself constitutes proof, and the inanimate object, although a dumb witness, becomes the only witness required against the accused citizen, thus establishing a prima-fascia case.

Because there is no way in which an inanimate object may be cross examined, the right contained within the Constitution to face, and cross examine your accuser, is totally negated.

This transfers the burden of proof from the state to prove guilt, to the accused citizen to prove innocence, an impossible, as well as unlawful task!

As the mere finding of an inanimate criminal carries the presumption of guilt, the likelihood of it having been "planted" is pervasive, thus, a stigma of corruption taints the justice process from its very outset.

How do you maintain the integrity, and thus trust in a justice system that can be totally manipulated by the police system, long before the accused sees the inside of a courtroom?

This Scenario Is Not a Presumption of What Might Transpire!

The so called "temperance" period in the nineteen twenties, resulted in the enactment of a Constitutional amendment, which created a nation of instant criminals, of previously law abiding citizens.

This amendment declared an inanimate object, alcohol, to be a criminal. Enabling legislation, resulted in laws allowing the court system to be totally bypassed.

The entire nation became not only subject to arrest, trial, and imprisonment, and the mere possession of this "criminal," reduced every citizen to the potential status of "acceptable sacrifice," as the badge of law enforcement, became a "license to kill."

What is so frightening is that this guilt by association apparently made perfect sense to the "educated leaders" of their day, and the "educated leaders" of our day, apparently learning nothing from history, are now forcing another dose of this government lawlessness down our throats.

Our prohibition era, is the best of many examples, of what occurs when government employees act without either compassion, or common sense.

Neighbor was suspicious of neighbor, police acting on tips and accusations, broke down doors in the middle of the night, violating personal and property rights at will, and with

impunity.

As might have been expected, who you knew, became far more important, than what you knew.

Violence was rampant! The new breed of true criminal organized and controlled entire cities, with the only aspect distinguishing them from the police, was the uniform.

This period in American history, laid the foundation for the current sweetheart deals between politicians, lawyers, judges, and organized crime, permeating to the very highest levels of government.

This reality, constructed over seventy years ago, and reaching to the very highest levels of our banking and financial structure, is being utilized and expanded to this day.

A "war" against an inanimate object, is a "war" against common justice, and common sense; yet we and our "leaders" appear to learn nothing.

The "war" on drugs, and prostitution, is occurring in almost exactly the same manner, and with exactly the same results; the corruption of government, and bastardization of the criminal justice system.

Absent the NRA, Guns Would Have Long Ago Taken Their Place On the Infamous List!

By design, our court system is to act as a buffer, and safeguard, between the legislative branch of government, and the individual citizen.

The courts are intended to act as a separate entity of government, not as a rubber stamp, enforcing any legislation which is either released, or manages to escape, from the halls of Congress.

The lack of commons sense, and restraint, in the enactment and enforcement of legislation by the people charged with safe guarding the rights, and well-being, of the individual citizen, is not only frightening, but, because it violates their oath, criminal.

The police now routinely violate all rules of assumed innocence; confiscating property without due process; splitting the seized money and property between the police and other government agencies; with the blessing of the highest court of the land; ***and we can't understand why we are treading water in a cess pool?***

How many times must history repeat, before we finally get this message: The Creation of Inanimate Criminals, Combined with Trial by Press, Guilt by Accusation, and Trial for Association, Debases, Thus Criminalizes, the Criminal Justice System!

An important aspect of my natural freedom, is my right to both defend myself, and to the means of accomplishing this task.

If I am faced with a situation in which I am threatened with either bodily harm, or death, then I am justified in assuming the threat to be the intent of my protagonist, and acting accordingly.

If armed, it is my choice to take the life of my adversary, without giving that adversary the opportunity to carry out the threat. It then becomes my duty, to justify my action, to the satisfaction of my fellow citizens.

The responsibility of my government, is to provide me a fair, and competent forum, in which to accomplish this act.

However, I don't feel that I enjoy the luxury of choice, if the life or welfare of my family, friends, or, even that of an innocent stranger is involved.

To do less than my best, and to use anything less than that available to me in defending these people, even at great risk to

my personal welfare, would be both cowardice, and a betrayal of my responsibility.

Am I unusual?

Just look at the record of your fellow Americans in a time of crisis. The names of men and women who have forfeited their lives, in defense of their fellow man, is legion.

Many police officers and firemen, although not required to intentionally risk certain death, have done so, as have our service people, and private citizens, and few have considered themselves hero.

Legions of teachers, lawyers, judges, and professors daily lend the credence of their education, to the argument that the right to the means of self protection is only within the context of an armed militia

Well Guess What?

This nation is inhabited by former military people, trained to be second to none, as we have proven on foreign soil.

When we "mustered out" of active service, only our bodies left; our training, as well as our oath of commitment to the security of this nation, will remain with most of us until our last breath.

We are citizen soldiers; a militia by every definition of the word, and these weapons will only be confiscated by military action; military personnel, against former military personnel; a potential blood bath to terrible to contemplate, but a certainty if an attempt is made to disarm us.

Very few of we the common people, possess the resources to make our voices heard over the millionaire and billionaire tycoons, both foreign and domestic, buying the influence of our "public servants!"

Why then, is it so surprising that we the people, in very large numbers, do not trust these *mistresses*, with total, and irrevocable control of our lives, as well as those of our children.

Why Not Take A Lesson From The Past?

It has never been necessary to "outlaw" and confiscate individually owned weapons. A very small percentage of Americans are really in love with guns; many of us, though in possession of concealed carry permits, seldom carry.

Once convinced that they could trust the courts to deliver justice, our ancestors enthusiastically put their weapons in the closet; the present generations have followed their lead.

Why do the judges, lawyers, and politicians, not perceive the direct correlation between the current weapons "problem," and the betrayal of that trust?

Are There Too Many Firearms In This Nation?

Even many adamant defenders of our right to these weapons, would answer in the affirmative.

Many of us also agree that weapons of any kind, have no place in certain locations.

The one fact with which we all agree however, is that: *In quantity, and duration, the time that these weapons spend in the closet, mirrors exactly the citizens perception of their need.*

The fulfilling of the promise of justice, and the creation and maintenance of conditions under which these weapons are not needed, is the duty of our representatives, to raid the closet where they are stored, Is Not!

Restore The Justice System, And The Gun "Problem" Vanishes!

ISRAEL

"Is life so dear, or peace so sweet, as to be purchased at the price of chains and slavery? Forbid it, Almighty God! I know not what course others my take, but as for me, give me liberty, or give me death." Patrick Henry

In The Course of Mans History, We Have Found Endless Reasons to Proclaim Elitism.

I am prettier than you, I am taller than you, I'm white and you're black, I have more wealth, I live in a higher culture, my ancestors came over on the Mayflower, etc.

However, The Ultimate Claim Is, "I'm Better Than You, Because My God Says That I'm Better Than You."

With this assertion, for thousands of years, the various Hebrew Tribes justified preemptive invasion, and total eradication of indigenous populations, as witnessed by their own hand!

The Old Testament, dedicated primarily to ancient Hebrew history, candidly details the structure, and lays bare their religious philosophy.

This history reveals war, destruction, conquest, and genocide. Entire nations destroyed, their lands confiscated, and their citizenry enslaved, for the purpose of building the various Hebrew "civilizations."

The whirlpool created by six thousand years of this seemingly endless cycle of violence and counter violence, continues to pull the human race ever deeper into the vortex of what could well be its extinction.

As our weapons daily become more lethal, to ignore the actions,

motivations, and repercussions, presented with pride, in such vivid detail, would be the height of folly.

Jewish history proves the wisdom of the statement: "That he who lives by the sword, shall die by the sword," yet the focus of the Hebrew religion, is the justification of the barbarity performed in the name, and supposedly by command, of Jehovah their God!

If true, Jehovah is, in every sense of the word, the war God of the Israelites, just as Mars was the war God of the Greeks.

According to the Old Testament, Jehovah's promise, all contingent upon unquestioned obedience to his commands, is eventual world domination by the Hebrew race, and utter damnation for all who oppose it!

Let's review the circumstances by which the Commandments that so many Jews, and Christians alike, would apparently love to see added to our Constitution, and displayed on every public building within the nation, came into existence.

The Jewish claim is that their status as "the chosen" prompted Jehovah too bind the nation with these laws.

However, these laws came into existence during the flight from their captivity in Egypt.

The scriptures themselves make it quite clear, that the Hebrew race of the time, totally devoid of self government, had degenerated into nothing but a mob. Quite interestingly, this fact brings too mind, the biblical quotation that: " Laws are created, not for the just, but for the unjust!"

As evidenced within the Bible itself, these laws were not intended too govern Hebrew conduct toward inferior races. Quite the contrary!

They were enacted for the purpose of governing the conduct between the various Hebrew tribes, thereby preserving what

little civility remained within an unruly mob!

Forget The Commandment "Though shalt not kill."

The Bible makes it quite clear that the Hebrew race was created for, dedicated to, became quite proficient at, and delighted in, the destruction of the perceived enemies, of Jehovah their God!

As is also borne out in the Christian Bible, this assertion has served as the catalyst for unspeakable brutality, death and destruction, a true testament to mans inhumanity to man.

Their proficiency in fact, resulted in the eradication of entire races, at the behest of Jehovah their God.

Modern Judaism is perceived to remain dedicated to this God of destruction; waiting and praying for the day that Jehovah will fulfill his promised subjection of all nations, to Jewish domination.

If biblical history is any indication of the planned future of the non Jewish residents of the planet, apprehension and mistrust is indeed in order.

Supposedly the Hebrew nation, or more accurately the Hebrew confederation, was born into, and remained dedicated to their concept of freedom for a number of years, prior to the establishment of the Hebrew Kingdom, a form of government which they were warned against.

We find in the first Book of Samuel, chapter eight of the Old Testament, Samuels description of the harm awaiting the Hebrew citizenry, upon embracing the ways of Monarchy, thereby departing from the ways of freedom.

Biblical history proves the wisdom of every statement!

This same book describes the behavior of Saul, a man made King over the Hebrews by Jehovah their God, however, we are also told, that Jehovah repented from, or regretted his anointed choice for King, and as the result Saul's reign was cut short by an untimely death.

Now a question!

Why would an all knowing being, perform an act, from which repentance would ultimately be required? Isn't the definition of sin, the performance of an act previously known to be wrong?

We also find in the Book of Samuel, that Saul was possessed by both good, and evil spirits emanating from God.

This bit of information elicits another question!

Why was I taught in church, that only good things come from God, and that all evil is from Satan?

Although one of the most depraved persons described in the Bible, even killing in mass, eighty five priest of Jehovah God, Saul was not brutal enough when dealing with the Amalekites, sparing the best sheep, and taking old King Agag alive.

David became King of the Hebrew nation following the death of Saul, and in the aftermath of a civil war; his conduct was no less deplorable.

He committed every sin, and broke every ordinance of civilized behavior, yet, if you believe the propaganda, because of his exalted position as King, he enjoyed Divine protection and praise, as "the man after Jehovah's own heart."

Amnon, one of the sons of David, asked Tamar, his sister for sex; she refused, stating that if he asked their father, the King, that he would not withhold her from him, he instead raped her.

And now another question!

Was incest so rampant within the Jewish culture, that it was

assumed common place to one of the Kings daughters?

The rape resulted in Absalom, another of David's sons, killing Amnon his brother, and rebelling against his father.

Rape, murder, and incest within the family of a man after Jehovah Gods own heart?

Now another question or two! How can a God not only accept, but glorify the total disregard of his own Commandments, by the leader of his chosen people?

How can anyone be proud to trace their linage back to this?

Born, following the untimely death of a sibling conceived in the adulterous relationship of David, and his mother Bathsheeba, a gentile woman for whom David arranged widowhood, Solomon's ascension to the Jewish throne, constituted gross violation of Hebrew law.

First because it passed over legitimate sons, and second, because it corrupted the linage.

The reign of Solomon has been pointed out with pride, by generations of Jews, as the epitome of wisdom and leadership, although he too lived a very immoral, and paganistic life.

In keeping with the axiom that: " Results prove or disprove, both theory and statement." or to put it another way "Proof of the pudding, is in the eating," I have a question!

If this man was so wise, and his leadership so brilliant, why was the nation in a state of civil war, and his sons at his throat, at the time of his death?

The answer is too be found in the book of Kings.

Why, within three generations, under the "royal" leadership of Saul, David and Solomon, the ordained representatives of

Jehovah God, did the Hebrew confederation cease to exists?

The answer: Over one hundred years of war, much of it among themselves!

Many were killed, some enslaved, others assimilated into conquering nations, however, of the twelve original tribes, only two maintained even a semblance of identity.

The narration of events contained within this book, if true, serves as very strong evidence that the Hebrew race, by intent of their God, must have been the most blood thirsty people to ever exist.

Indeed when Samuel asked why they wanted a King, the reply was: "To Lead Us In War!" An intent realized!

Saul, their first king we are told in the Holy word of Jehovah, was very envious of David. It seems that while the people were celebrating the thousands killed by his hand, they were celebrating the tens of thousands who died at the hand of David.

While we are condemning and vilifying an Arab leader for aggression in 1990's, and deservedly so, we cannot escape the fact that in the late 1940's, the United States and Great Britain, were instrumental in the reassembly of this egotistical, and bloody race.

The United States governments current role as mediator of the Middle East crisis, loses its luster, when that of facilitator, our initial role, is taken into account.

In the late nineteen forties, the State of Israel, at the behest, and with the funding of the US government, was legally, although unlawfully created by the United Nations, in what is proving to be the most strategic place on the planet.

In a region with at least a six thousand year history of almost constant religious warfare and genocide, the United States, by

assisting in the "partitioning" (taking) of land belonging to one of the combatants, and awarding it to another, exacerbated these old hatreds.

By providing the staging area, prodigious quantities of money, state of the art weaponry and training, our contribution to this historically unstable quagmire, has in reality been the creation of a ticking time bomb, a bomb which is now thermonuclear!

For at least the last fifty years, anyone attempting a critique, or offering criticism of either ancient, or, contemporary Hebrew conduct, although detailed within the Christian Bible, and displayed daily on the current world stage, has been very vociferously labeled "anti-Semitic," by the Jewish Anti Defamation League.

I have no doubt that I, and this essay, will be added to the list. However, it is my good fortune to have been born in a nation, whose Supreme Law guarantees my right to offer an honest assessment of a book, with which I have spent untold hours in contemplative study.

Fact! We confiscated the ancestral homeland of an indigenous people, and gave it to immigrants, as well as a continuous supply of weapons and money with which to hold the property with military power.

Fact! The inhabitants instantly, and unjustly, acquired the status of inferior beings, and were expelled from, or, incarcerated in, the nation of their birth.

Fact! Reduced to the status of refugees, a people without a country, the determinant of their very existence, became the generosity and acceptance of neighboring nations.

There is no escaping our culpability in the creation of this cancer of animosity now destroying many innocent lives; destabilizing the entire Middle East; and greatly contributing too our national shame, as well as national debt.

Our Reward?

Israel maintains a constant spying operation, within our nation.

Knowingly, and viciously attacked the Liberty, one of our ships, killing many sailors.

Is claiming the right to murder those suspected of being enemies of Israel, *Within Our Nations Borders.*

Suborns the subversion of our government, while unlawfully acquiring, and maintaining, an arsenal of weapons of mass destruction.

The acts committed against the indigenous Arab population in the late 1940's, is even more heinous than those committed against our citizens of Japanese heritage in the early 1940's.

A war provided a facade of justification, for the American governments atrocious act of stripping citizens of Japanese heritage of their citizenship, property, dignity, and freedom.

Justification in any form, has never existed for similar acts perpetrated against the Arabs, nor for United States involvement in the creation and continued support, of a religiously, and ethnically segregated, Israeli State.

Our theft of a peoples ancestral birthrights, and the condemnation of their following generations to perpetual homelessness, not in our nation, but in their own, for the purpose of Subjecting Them Too Conduct and Conditions, That We The People Of The United States Would Not Tolerate, is Despicable!

How Can We Blame Them For Their Hatred?

Let's take look at the situation, from some different perspectives.

Supposing the indigenous population of the area to be Jewish, with a history of possession of the land for two thousand years; what would have been the result, had the same land been confiscated, and the affected citizens confined in displaced persons camps, for the purpose of creating a Muslim State?

How would the United States now be viewed by Jews all over the world?

Would we not consider the American government the big Satan, had it decreed in 1948 that the Far Eastern part of California, and perhaps the Western part of Nevada, would become the new Zionist governed homeland, of World Judaism.

All residents of the confiscated land, unless Jewish, after being deprived of their citizenship, property, vote, and civil rights, would forthwith be confined in displaced persons camps, or, on the assumption that the neighboring states would welcome their new citizens with open arms, those who preferred, would be allowed to emigrate to Oregon, Nevada, Utah, and Arizona.

Meanwhile, Jews from around the world would not only be welcomed into their new home, but would be provided with a continuous supply of food; the latest in weaponry, including tanks and aircraft; as well as several billion dollars per year, courtesy of the United States taxpayers.

And of course, if, in their minds, their security was ever threatened, or, perhaps in the need of water, they could use the American furnished weapons too "annex" the west bank of Lake Tahoe, and even lay waste too, or occupy Reno--all the while, developing weapons of mass destruction, including thermonuclear capability.

Had these events occurred, would the Christian citizenry of the United States, have displayed any more compassion toward the Jews than that which the Arab Muslim have shown, or, would the United States have erupted into immediate civil war, with every

politician on the run for their lives?

We Are All Very Cognizant of That Answer!

Just how did the US get roped into this patently unlawful act?

The answer!

Fantastically wealthy Jewish financiers, (Rothschild's) playing upon the sympathy for the survivors of the Jewish slaughter during the Second World War, influenced the implementation of a plan previously concocted by Great Britain.

During the intervening two thousand years, has the Jews perspective of their status as Gods Chosen People changed?

How about their contention that: By God The Land Belongs To Them; And By God They Will Possess It By Any Means Available?

The answers are revealed in the following statements.

David Ben Gurion, Jewish Labor Party leader/terrorist in 1937 stated: *"The acceptance of partition does not commit us to renounce Trans Jordan; one does not demand from anybody to give up his vision. We shall accept a state in the boundaries fixed today, but the boundaries of Zionist aspirations are the concern of the Jewish people, and no external factor will be able to limit them."* close quote

David Ben Gurion again in 1938: " *After we become a strong force, as the result of the creation of a state, we shall abolish partition and expand to the whole of Palestine. The state will only be a stage in the realization of Zionism, and its task is to prepare the ground for our expansion into the whole of Palestine, by Jewish-Arab agreement... The state will have to preserve order not only by preaching morality, but by machine guns, if necessary."* close quote

Following the establishment of the state in 1948 Menachem Begin stated that: *"The partition of the Homeland is illegal. It will never be recognized. The signature of institutions and individuals of the partition agreement is invalid. It will not bind the Jewish people. Jerusalem was and will forever be our capital. Eretz Israel will be restored to the people of Israel. All of it. And forever."* close quote (all emphasis added) * From Fateful Triangle -- Noam Chomsky

Even with a thirty year record of murders, massacres, assassinations and bombings, from both antagonist, the leadership of the United States, committed endless prestige and resources, to this twentieth century Crusade.

The details will never be known, however, it is quite likely that the Banksters, in the guise of the Federal Reserve, having acquired control of the American treasury in December of 1913, made Congress a deal which they literally couldn't refuse.

How it occurred at this stage of the game is immaterial, the fact remains, that for over fifty years, we have furnished Israel the necessary resources for atrocities, had they been committed in our nation, would have subjected the perpetrators to prison sentences or execution!

The state of Israel remains the haunting personification of our hypocrisy!

Six hundred and fifty thousand men died in the Civil War, setting the stage for the ultimate eradication of discrimination within our nation, the product of segregation.

"Partitioning" of "The Holy Land," amounts to nothing more than the alternate spelling of segregation, in an effort directed toward the camouflaging of the practice of discrimination.

The expending of a lot of hard work, aimed at stamping out the practice, while repairing the damage, and reversing the affects, of better than one hundred years of sorrow, and shame, its

product; while simultaneously creating a new nation rooted in the same, discredited philosophy, must qualify as the personification of stupidity.

Another very disturbing Israeli practice, is the assumption of the right to initiate preemptive acts of war, in any instance, when, in their opinion, their national security or interest are threatened; a philosophy adopted by, and recently utilized by the United States in initiating the Iraqi War.

In light of this, this question must be asked: Will the military slaughter of American citizens be condoned, should things turn nasty, as the result of our impending financial collapse?

If we will justify and finance it in a foreign country, why is this not a very justifiable question?

Also, it is no secret that Christianity is a derivative of Judaism, thus, those of my fellow citizens who insist that the United States was founded a Judeo/Christian nation, and would love to have the Ten Commandments adopted and promoted by our government, is itself disturbing.

It is very difficult for many citizens too accept, but our Constitutional guarantee of freedom of religion, also translates as freedom from religion!

The driving force behind the formation of the United States, was the entitlement to freedom of thought and action, regardless of religious persuasion.

If an individual desires the benefits described by the priest, rabbi, or preacher, and is convinced that he, or, they can deliver those benefits, then it is their right to submit to any course of action prescribed, by that particular individual, or, organization.

However, if I neither desire that being offered, nor believe that the person or organization offering those benefits can deliver,

then it is within my rights, to decline to participate.

Our national policy of the separation of church and state, does not even allow the government representatives, to promote these unproven claims.

As a Jewish American, do you support action repugnant to the founding principles of the United States? If so, anything which you demand as a citizen of this nation, and would deny someone else in another land, screams hypocrisy.

Do you, a Catholic American, support the claim that the Pope is God ordained royalty, and the Cardinals, Princes of the royal court?

If you are working at destroying the barrier between church and state, barriers that encompass the right of free speech as well as the right of free association and assembly, you are chipping away at the very foundation of this nation.

These are only two examples of actions tearing the very heart out of this nation. There are many individuals, groups, and organizations, who desire nothing less than having their fellow citizens bound to their definition of freedom, and their version of religion.

It is not my desire to offend anyone, nor is it to provoke hatred, quite the contrary, it is to provoke thought.

If the citizens of the state of Israel choose to build a prison for themselves, in a country alive with their avowed enemies, that is their prerogative.

If they choose to pay the price in money and lives to perpetuate this living arrangement, that is also their prerogative.

You would think however, that after thousands of years, the fallacy of the idea of the road to peace, running through the valley of hate and elitism, would have gotten through to them.

Is it too much to expect me, as well as many other citizens of this nation, to decline to participate in anyway, but especially to refuse to furnish money or weapons to be used to perpetuate practices abhorrent to the principles of our own Declaration of Independence?

How can we condemn the conduct of governments in other nations, while financing the same conduct in Israel?

Our leaders, Christian and otherwise, vociferously denounce the lack of civility and respect for human life supposedly typical of the Moslem religion, yet conveniently overlook several hundred years of Christian Crusades and Inquisitions, and the resulting slaughter of an estimated fifty million, primarily Moslem people.

Likewise, while leaders of the present nation of Israel bemoan the savagery, and feign lack of understanding for the propensity of the Palestinian people to become suicide bombers, they conveniently overlook thousands of years of their own barbaric history.

The founding of the present state of Israel, on land stolen by the UN from its Moslem inhabitants, and their condemnation to the perpetual hopelessness of refugee status, should explain something.

Revisiting the words of Patrick Henry: Perhaps Suicide Bombings?

Many years ago I was listening to a radio broadcast in which Moshe Dayan, a prominent Israeli of the time, was being interviewed.

His response to the question of whether or not the Jews still possess the Masada Complex, obviously referring too the incident in Jewish history, in which hatred, plus futility and hopelessness, equated to mass suicide.

His response: No! They now possess the Sampson complex, meaning that they will take as many people with them as possible, ala Sampson's feat of collapsing the stadium upon himself, as well as his antagonist.

This insight leaves little doubt, that had the opportunity existed, the Jews would have been delighted to have taken as many Romans with themselves as possible at Masada.

What is frightening, is the fact that they now possess enough weapons of mass destruction, to, of not wipe out the earths population, to at least condemn the survivors to a living hell.

It seems also, that not so long ago, right here in the United States, I recall the slogan: "better dead than red," equating quite clearly, the futility of life, commensurate with the loss of freedom.

Does anyone experience any doubt, that the United States would have employed the arsenal of doomsday weapons at our disposal then, nor those we possess today, should the choice become captivity or death?

The leaders of the Soviet Union certainly didn't!

Freedom or death is still very much alive in the USA, why then is it such a shock, that the same concept lives in Arab hearts as well?

<u>In Summery!</u>

My God is a God of creation, and I resent having the funds which I earn by peaceful means, employing the abilities granted me by that God, being utilized to supply the weapons and ammunition to kill people rendered homeless and defenseless by my government.

The enormous wealth supplied Israel over the last fifty years, allowing them to mock the principles of the Declaration of Independence, has cost this nation far more than its monetary value.

The indoctrination that the American people have received, camouflaging the hypocrisy of the deed, has been so successful, that many people accept it as truth, not even considering the true facts, and weighing them against the principles most of us espouse.

We, as a nation, have been demonstrating for peace, expecting our leaders to listen, wave a magic wand, and presto we have our wish.

The hard truth is, the option for peace does not rest with our nation. We destroyed our credibility as peace ambassadors, when we violated the civil rights, and human dignity, of the Palestinian people.

By dignifying the Jewish claim of racial and religious elitism, we guaranteed perpetual conflict, and a well deserved enmity toward ourselves.

If I, as an individual, took your home by force and gave it to my friend, I would be guilty of theft. The fact that I controlled the legal system, and thus escaped punishment for the crime, would in no way alter the fact of my guilt.

If I furnished the means to the power for my friend to retain possession of your home, and left you in the street, it would serve as a constant reminder that I was your enemy.

If, at some point in time I no longer had the power to protect my friend, you no doubt would reclaim your property, and, if the situation presented itself, would not hesitate to inflict punishment to me.

Why are people who resent being robbed considered terrorist if they employ secret military action against the robber, knowing

that an open demonstration will result in there being beaten, and to pick up a stone, might well result in their death?

Have we set the stage for Armageddon?

By providing land stolen from traditional enemies--in the midst of what is proving to be the most strategic and sensitive area on planet earth--providing the latest in weaponry, as well as a continuous and ample supply of money--we have certainly assembled the ingredients.

EPILOG

As previously stated, this book was not written nor published for the purpose of making anyone mad, generating hatred, nor changing minds, contrarily, its purpose was that of provoking thought; controversy; and discussion!

There are few thinking people within this nation who do not recognize the fact that we not only must, but are even now, in the midst of radical change.

THE EIGHT HUNDRED POUND GORILLA

The strength of the American dollar, and its acceptance as currency of account in world trade, derives from one thing, the strength and dominance of our military, and our willingness, and at times, eagerness, too project that strength

That statement was certainly no masterpiece of brilliance!

There can be no better testimony than our wealth and living standard, to the fact that we the American people, have, in the aftermath of world war, profited immensely from that fortuitous, all be it, catastrophic event.

It is also quite clear, that a very large percentage of the worlds population has, as the result of a half century of stable currency; the promotion of personal freedom; and an explosion of trade; also prospered.

Until recently, the question, "*where does an eight hundred pound gorilla sleep*" has always been answered with: "anywhere he so chooses!"

However, when the recently added previso, "if he expects to awaken hale and hearty," is added--assuming a smart gorilla; before the question may be answered, many new aspects, must be factored in.

EPILOG

Obviously, the foremost aspect, must be the emotion evoked by his reputation among the majority of the inhabitants of his recently chosen bedroom.

Is it Hate; Fear; Grudging Acceptance; or, a Transitory Sense of Futility?

Concurrent with the transitory change of attitude toward the gorilla, from, *love*, through *futile acceptance*, into *avid hatred*, in the span of forty plus years, the government has transitioned from *surplus, through, millions ; billions; and into, according to some estimates, in excess of twenty trillion,* dollars of debt!

Mere Coincidence?

What ever the true total, great effort, deception, and creative accounting methods, have been employed by government, for the purpose of its concealment, with no thought of remedy.

With a government hemorrhaging red ink; the relative value of exports compared to imports daily deteriorating; and a population adamantly refusing to increase their tax burden, even to fund local schools, the truth can no longer be avoided.

Ad the shortage of required revenue at every level, from the smallest community, to the largest state government, and it certainly requires no soothsayer, to deduce the obvious:

A Nation On A Collision Course With The Reality Of Either Inflation Or Depression, Of Massive Scale!

The debt will be repudiated, either before or after blood runs in the street; Hopefully Before!

The economic system, as detailed within the Constitution, was not designed for the purpose of controlling the citizenry, either in mass, or individually!

Contrarily, it assigned the duty of issuing and maintaining the value of the currency to those chosen from our ranks, for the purpose of representing our interest in the affairs of state.

The substance of which the currency was to be created was specified as gold and silver, with purity also specified at ninety percent.

By merely determining and maintaining the value of the metal, in direct correlation with the quantity, the system, as designed, would run on auto pilot.

How could a system have been better devised than that?

Granted, gold and silver was in such short supply, that it was destined to very quickly prove inadequate for the job.

As technologically created wealth forged a life style that no quantity of gold could equal in value, and no way of adequately applying its true value to the economic system, a new system was inevitable.

Although the plan for the asset based system had been finalized, and put into place by Congress and President Wilson in December 1913, the nation transitioned through a system identified by the letters GNP, an acronym for gross national product.

The new system was composed of the wealth produced by the combination of the nations labor, genius, management, automated production, and the export of food, fiber, and natural resources.

Success not only breeds success, but in this case, because there was nothing to be gained by the manipulation of either production or valuation figures--*honesty*!

The honestly calculated new wealth, adding daily to the US economic system, supplied both impetus and motivation, to the

creation of additional wealth beyond measure.

As real work, contributed real wealth to the economy, gold and silver certificates served the role of proxies, very admirably. As previously noted however, it was merely a transitory period, in the nations journey into corporate finance, *The Economic System From Hell*.

From the time the Corporate System opened its doors, silver certificates, and Federal Reserve Notes, circulated simultaneously as well as interchangeably, thus, We The People were unaware of either their origin, or, pedigree.

When the silver coins, and silver certificates, were removed from circulation, none of us, by intent, thought anything about it. The Federal Reserve notes had been, also by plan, created in abundance, and were thus very plentiful.

The corporate system, chartered in 1913 by the Democratic government of Woodrow Wilson, was literally a license to print, circulate, and profit, from money printed against the assets of the nation itself.

Translation: Each note was, and is, a portion of title too the land, and resources, as well as all common wealth, either previously created, or too be created, Into Perpetuity!

Our Nation Was Sold Out, By "Damn-ocratic" Government!

The monetary cancer has, over a period of years, been so thoroughly integrated into the US economic system, that for all practical purposes, *on paper*, The "Fed" now owns title to not only the government, but the nation itself.

Imagine for a moment that the door bell rings at a family home. Upon answering it, the man of the house is greeted with:

"Great News Mr. Lucky, You Have Just Inherited an Interest in a Thriving Construction Company!"

EPILOG

It is located in a new neighborhood, is totally equipped with the latest equipment, shops, offices, trucks, material etc. and is staffed by some very industrious workers, fellow employees who are also your partners.

Although knowing nothing about construction, his expertise and inherited interests, seemingly qualifies him for a position in management.

Thus Mr. Lucky, an attorney, is welcomed to the board of directors of a company, who, from engineer to janitor, are tops in their field.

After a few weeks on the job, he has an inspiration for a new name and logo, "United Construction." The board approves, and very shortly all the signs, advertising, and contracts, proudly bear that name.

Because his expertise is seldom required, his greatest contribution is in not interfering with his fellow partner/employees. However, he gets a great thrill just touring his new place of residence, showing off his new pickup, with "his" new company name prominently displayed.

With the assumption that he and his family deserve a change in life style, he encounters a small problem. It seems that although the business is thriving, and is virtually free of debt, the profits have been plowed back into the business. Every available dollar is allotted to the purpose of increasing the strength and value of the company.

While each partner/employee, according to their value to the company, is taking enough salary out of the business for a comfortable living, those who desire more elegant surrounding, are expected to acquire greater proficiency and education, thereby increasing their value to the company, thus deservedly, an increase in salary.

EPILOG

Mr. Lucky reasons that his "position in management" does indeed dictate a little more extravagant lifestyle than those in "labor," so, although aware of the cost of financing his new life style, elects to go for it.

The construction business, far harder than Mr. Lucky had supposed, and his management skills far less than adequate, after losing considerable money, discovered that he was incapable of correctly bidding work. Oh well, he would just assign that work to "his" employees, he much preferred to just be seen in his new company truck anyway.

Mr. Lucky, as the result of interest payments, watched as the disposable value of his salary decreased precipitously. Aware that his contribution to the business was virtually nil, but unable to "find" the time to acquire new skills, he realized that he dare not ask the board of directors for an increase in salary.

So, in his capacity as chief financial officer, he began taking increasing amounts of money from the company, while, with innovative book keeping and the creative language of an attorney, hiding the withdrawals from his partner/managers.

Meanwhile, with unlimited innovation and dedication, the company was booming, thus, the rapidly increasing wealth, as well as the increasingly creative language, served to hide Mr. Lucky's proclivity as a master thief, very well.

Although he still had ties to the old neighborhood, for the most part he and the company tried to stay out of their problems, only occasionally getting involved in an effort toward quelling their seemingly constant squabbles; his new found success however, was not going unnoticed by his old friends.

In addition, Mr. Lucky's life style was being looked upon with envy by some employees, especially a few of his co-managers, several of whom had become close friends.

Circumstances dictating that he take some of them into his confidence, he thus revealed a proposal which had been tendered by some seemingly very wealthy men in the old neighborhood, people to whom he himself owed his "success" as well as much of his salary.

He explained their offer of a new company financial system, the one which their ancestors had made available to managers in the old neighborhood many years previously.

No longer would they be restricted by cash flow or production efficiency, they would just write checks, send them to their bank, and the bank would provide the funding.

There was only one catch! There was a charge for their services, and to secure payment, the Managers must Give the Bank a Lien on All Company Assets.

Mr. Lucky's new confidants however saw only: Unlimited Money Supply: No More Worry about Finances: Occasional "Bonus" for Each of the Manager/Directors: "WOW," what a deal!

Aware of restrictions placed upon their authority by the company charter, one of which was denial of the right to incur debt without approval of the board of directors, and equally aware, that should the word get out, many of the frugal employee/owners would ask some very embarrassing and difficult questions, it went without saying that: Details of the Deal, Would Be Revealed Only on a Need to Know Basis!

Thus, one day when members of the board of directors, feared to oppose the new arrangement, were absent, those in the know quietly asked, where do we sign? The conspiracy was concluded!

United Construction now owned its own bank "United Financial Inc," or so the partner/employees were led to believe.

Suddenly the company was awash in cash. The employees had no idea why it occurred, however, with complete trust in their fellow employee/managers, most were not concerned. The company seemingly was doing fantastic, many got raises, and thus could afford to borrow on their future earnings, while "investing" in "the market.

" Times, They Were A Roaring!

"United Financial Inc," like the proverbial goose, appeared to be laying golden eggs.

However, a few short years into the miracle, a major financial crisis severely crippled the company. Many of the partner/employees watched helplessly as their seemingly endless prosperity vanished, replaced with destitution.

Things were bleak for several years, ending only as the result of a major squabble in the old neighborhood; another crisis which necessitated their assistance.

In addition to man power, that assistance required an immediate, expansive growth of every division: transportation, communication, health care, equipment manufacturing, food production, armaments etc. you name it, United Construction was into it in a big way.

Eventually the problem was solved, or at least quelled, and miraculously the company financial crisis had vanished, and just as miraculously, the expansion not only continued unabated, but intensified; company wealth productivity went off the scale.

A revitalized, "United Financial Inc." continued to pump out funding upon request for anything desired, mergers, buyouts, import/exports, security, research and development, venture capital etc. again, you name it and "United Financial Inc." would provide the funds, for a Fee, Guaranteed by Title to the Project or Business, of Course!

The same was true for the employee/partners private lives;

anything desired, houses, cars, boats, anything, could be attained instantly at the many locations of "United Financial Inc." Again for a Fee Guaranteed by Title.

United Construction was flooding the world with food and merchandise, and "United Financial Inc." with funds to purchase them.

Although it didn't make sense to some of the partner/employees to furnish the funds with which to purchase the products, few gave it any thought. People in the old neighborhood needed the merchandise, and the partner/employees of United Construction, needed a market for their excess production.

<u>Happy Days Were Here Again!</u>

"Professional management," top heavy in lawyers I might add, who had long since replaced the original employee/partner/ management, came up with a brilliant idea: Why not have the items manufactured by people from the old neighborhood and import them, after all, they would work for virtually slave labor wages.

Although initially, the quality many times was lacking, too their delight, the partner/employees discovered that they could buy finished products, of at least suitable quality, for less than the cost of their own labor.

Although there were signs produced by some of their fellow partner/employees urging their fellow employees to "BUY UNITED PRODUCTS" most were of the opinion that management had indeed produced utopia, while in reality, the policies of management were increasing the difficulty of buying "UNITED PRODUCTS," either at home or abroad!

<u>As local manufacturing jobs, became foreign manufacturing jobs, the local facilities no longer needed, were either abandoned or sold.</u>

Many of the imported products required repackaging, and the robust sales of natural resources and food required labor, thus, for a short time, forestry, mining, farming etc. was still booming.

The added complexity and red tape required an enormous amount of record keeping, thus many employee/partners, were absorbed by "management," especially in the burgeoning security and legal divisions.

It seems professional management had determined that security personnel, previously deemed to be the responsibility of the male members of the company, randomly chosen and pressed into service as needed, would be replaced with professionals.

These dedicated professionals could then be quickly dispatched too protect the companies "best interest" at any location deemed threatened.

The really hot segments however were "United Financial Inc." and Law Suits Inc.

It seems they worked round the clock devising new uses for their services, thus, far more new partner/employees trained for, and sought employment in one of their many divisions.

They were also busy creating more rules arbitrarily restricting conduct, ownership, and even possession of certain materials deemed inappropriate or harmful for fellow partner/employees, even to the mandating of punishment.

Incarceration/punishment, absorbing huge amounts of revenue, became a growth industry.

Requiring increasing numbers of personnel, equipment, food, health care, and of course structure, it became a dead drain on company finances.

Meanwhile, company management absorbed many of the

EPILOG

"Experts in the Law" being produced by United Constructions schools, under the tutelage of "United Financials Inc."

Law Suits Inc. though producing nothing of intrinsic value, provided "work" for the surplus graduates.

Concentrating on "shaking down" any individual or enterprise they deemed to have "deep pockets," they honed the bourgeoning occupation of legal theft, to a fine art.

By increasing their funding at critical intervals, through the election process, "United Financial Inc." from the time of the financial crises, had begun purchasing even more seats on the board of directors of United Construction, eventually acquiring total control, and, again with targeted funding, continued to staff, (or is the term stuff) them with members of their choice.

What a Sweet Deal!

The board of United Construction determined how the "companies money" should be spent, and the board of "United Financial Inc." how and when it would be created, thus, the no longer needed partner/ laborers, (or so it seemed) were of very little concern.

The plates of the law and currency manipulators were heaped to overflowing, as were those for whom "United Financial Inc." in the name of the board of directors of United Construction, had written very favorable financial rules.

These rules, written in a language foreign too the vast majority of the employee/partners, were in a constant state of revision, thus, their "interpretation" and application, become a major industry.

And the partner /laborers?

They were welcome to that which "trickled down."

Correction! They Were Welcome to That Portion of it Which "United Financial Inc." Was Unsuccessful in Confiscating.

As the result, the law and currency manipulators got progressively richer, and the average partner/employee got screwed.

Although many employees screamed that the term was rape, the company "arbitrators," concurred with the constant propaganda blitz, and an occasional kiss from the board of directors of United Construction, who insisted that it was consensual.

Never the less, most of the partner/employees recognized rape when confronted with it, and many of its victims, by necessity, joined the rapidly evolving service industry, doing each others laundry, cooking, gardening etc. while trying desperately, too avoid even the occasional kiss.

However, every time "United Financial Inc." whether by theft, error, or greed, suffered any loss of revenue, from past experiences, the partner/employees knew that the board of United Construction would simply transfer the loss to them, therefore, many just laid down and spread their legs.

As could be expected, the company began to have trouble keeping work that justified paying the employee/partners enough to support themselves in the manner to which they had become accustomed, and eventually, even enough to secure basic necessities.

Producing little to export, the former owners/partners found themselves predominately in the import business, paying for virtually everything they consumed with IOU's, backed by the assets of United Construction, their former company

The result obviously, was a greater reliance on the services of "United Financial Inc." They just kept laying out the cash, and acquiring title to increasing quantities of the partner/employees future time.

EPILOG

Although going unrecognized, "United Financial Inc." on paper, had, long ago acquired United Construction, lock, stock, and barrel, as well as the employee/owners future.

Adding insult to injury, former contractors from the old neighborhood, had served their apprenticeships, learned their lessons well, and hungered for a better standard of living.

Thus, financially handicapped, United Construction, now found itself facing formidable competition from new businesses springing up world wide, while lacking the resources to even get back into the game.

Contrarily, through superb planning, management, and fraud, "United Financial Inc." had acquired "title" to virtually everything they touched.

For nothing more than the cost of printing paper money and "backing" financial contracts, they not only owned United Construction, but seemingly controlled the prosperity of much of the world.

However, there was trouble in paradise. Their system had become a doomsday machine.

They now owned title to all the company assets; the paper title to most everything the former employee/partners had previously owned, their future time, and the time of several generations of children yet unborn, <u>there was little left to borrow against!</u>

The system had itself become a dam, and without rapid circulation of the currency, the means by which critical funds were added to the "economy," <u>The System Quit Working Properly!</u>

Under their debt money system, it was becoming very difficult to supply adequate funds to the average employee/partner, without reducing its value precipitously, and, as they were discovering,

"mere laborers" were critical to the survival of the system.

They were also being challenged by several new financial systems; one in particular, New Banking System Limited, was already making serious inroads into their domain.

Many employee/partners were destitute, all in serious trouble, yet, the knowledge that their problems were rooted in a bogus business arrangement consummated 90 years previously, remained a mystery to most of them.

By camouflaging United Constructions financial arrangement with "United Financial Inc." and pyramiding the debt load under a blanket of deception, lies, and creative language, "management" had constructed a time bomb.

The "new money system" was beset with a small problem--it seems that the more "dollars" produced, the less they were worth.

Too mask this fact, rather than requiring the employee/owners, to fund company expenses as they were incurred, the management of United Construction, began borrowing the "dollars" required for operating expenses, from "United Financial Inc."

By hocking assets, assigning title to all company commonwealth to "United Financial Inc." while requiring the employees to fund only the customary fee, management could hide the true cost of operation, while assuring the partner/employees, that their money was not losing its value.

While the lie successfully hid the true rate at which their "new money" was shedding its value, the perpetually pyramiding debt, was rapidly multiplying the "customary fee," devouring revenue at a prodigious rate.

As the result of this betrayal of trust, the employee/partners did not demand wage increases commensurate with the lost value of

the "dollar," thus, eventually found themselves facing a debt denominated in the bogus "dollars," but without access to enough of them to even keep pace with the rapidly increasing prices of daily necessities.

The Miracle of the Perpetual Money Machine Was Revealed!

The original "arrangement, " had been perpetrated by fraud; a collusion between crooked company employee/partners, and a centuries old syndicate of professional con men.

A syndicate, which from the beginning, had no intention of working within the bounds of the company charter.

The "arrangement" had since been continuously perpetuated, by "professional management. "

The Granddaddy and Most Successful of All Ponzie Schemes!

Although Aware of the Old Truism That "Time Is Money, " Trust in Management Had Blinded Them to the Fact That Control of the Money System, Directly Equated to the Value of Their Time, and Control of Their Lives!
****

Obviously a summary of my contention that "Professional Management," through contempt for the time of "common labor," has created conditions under which the reorganization of not only the economic system, but government itself is unavoidable.

Can anyone think of any reason, that our elected representatives would abrogate their Constitutional responsibility of issuing and determining the value of our nations money, as well as maintaining its also Constitutionally mandated base of gold and silver?

The value of money, exchanged as a proxy of tangible wealth, must maintain its value beyond question, or even suspicion,

otherwise, it is not money.

The Articles of Confederation, the original document under which the Nation was formed, failed to establish a common currency fulfilling these requirements.

Continental currency, paper "money," circulated throughout the new nation; its acceptance as well as its "official" value was mandated by law. However, unofficially, its value, as well as its acceptance--succinctly summed up as: "Not Worth a Continental."

Needless to say it was not trusted in international trade.

Ironically, its acceptance as a novelty, was to eventually exceed its acceptance as a currency.

After the Articles of Confederation were replaced with the Constitution, and the "Continental" with gold and silver, the discredited currency, was often used as wall paper.

That which the British Army could not accomplish, paper money not only could, but was in the process of accomplishing.

Our forefathers recognized the source of the problem, and committed themselves to the task correcting it.

Now, just as then, the nation which no army in the world can subjugate, finds itself facing the same problems, and for the same reasons!

Betrayed ninety years ago, by representatives of our own "DAMN-OCRATIC" government, we are entering the final stages of subjugation, to the perpetrators of the most brazen, and elaborate con job, the world has ever seen.

It is very tempting to exclaim, as did Patrick Henry, over two hundred years ago, "Forbid it Almighty God!"

EPILOG

However, our fate, as was that of our forefathers, is in our own very capable hands, not those of an omnipotent being; thus the responsibility for our welfare, belongs to we, and we alone.

The nation, very early in its existence, was faced with a problem which could only be solved with real money, gold and silver.

Why Reinvent The Wheel?

The perils now facing our nation, are rooted in paper money , as was those of our forefathers.

Common problem, common remedy, return to the system devised and successfully employed.

Congress was assigned the responsibility of establishing the commodity money system, and maintaining its value, by the Constitution. Thus the currency act of 1792.

A Constitutional Convention is neither needed nor desired. The plan is there, and everyone of our government representatives have taken an oath to follow it; the only thing required, is that the oaths be honored!

Our Damn-ocratic government has imprisoned our following generation in a straitjacket of debt; This Fact Is Beyond Question, thus, we do not need committees or commissions to study the problem to death.
The Choice Is Ours!

Will we continue to devote prodigious quantities of our time, vicariously experiencing the excitement of "real life adventures," manufactured too be enjoyed in the comfort of our living rooms?

Or, through political activism, and the ballot box, re-establish control of our lives!

I can't do it, and neither can you, or you, or you.......but

together, it can become the reality of the land.

For starters, what we require is:

An immediate, absolutely honest, balanced, and definitive budget; followed by a balanced budget amendment to the Constitution, within one Presidential election cycle:

The focus of the Internal Revenue Service, too shift from the providers of the revenue, to those with whom it is entrusted:

The source of all federal revenue, will, within one Presidential election cycle, revert to the method established by the Constitution:

The Federal Reserve, following a definitive audit, will be restricted to private business, and will furnish a plan for the fulfillment of all outstanding obligations, or face liquidation:

Except as a verifiable act of self preservation, the power to declare war, or commit troops, will vest entirely with the Congress. Any military action the people are not willing to immediately fund, will not be engaged in:

The Focus Of Constitutional Interpretation, Will Shift From The Rights Of Government, To The Rights Of The Individual Citizen, Thus The Establishment Of A Constitutional Republic, As Guaranteed By That Document:

Our Journey Toward Individual Sovereignty

Will Have Begun!

NOT THE END, A NEW BEGINNIG!

I previously asked if anyone could think of any reason, that our government, endowed with the privilege of taxation, would borrow operating revenue, and then utilize that privilege to merely pay the perpetually accruing interest on the loan.

The answer is: Because the *current system* provides the *current law manipulators,* immediate, and unfettered access too seemingly unlimited treasure, as they hock the nations previously acquired assets, those currently being acquired, and those too be acquired, into perpetuity.

The obvious result, of the unholy alliance between the Currency and the Law Manipulators, is the binding of the nations following generations, in the chains of debt. Damnocratic Government, In Its Truest Form.

There is nothing wrong with *any government*, by *any name,* providing *any services*, that the current beneficiaries of those services are willing too *immediately* pay for. This reality institutes, and maintains, an honest political environment, within which government must function.

It is truly a government of the people, by the people, and for the people; Republican Government, In Its Truest Form.

What is being conclusively proven within our nation, is the fact that the practitioners of the political profession, cannot be trusted with the financial well-being of the nation, nor with its following generations future.

Our nations government was constructed a triad; three branches; each of which would serve too check and balance the power of the other.

The success of the system was contingent upon at least one of the three, at any given time, being staffed by citizens of high

integrity; jealously maintaining the principles, of Constitutional government.

When personal integrity, and sense of the honor bestowed upon them by their fellow citizens, became non-existent, and their collective desire mutated into the quest for personal aggrandizement:

When the elected offices became commodities, with its occupant in a continuous, "Let's Make A Deal" mind set:

When "Protection of Marriage" became top priority, while the binding of our children and grand children in the chains of perpetual debt became acceptable:

When our political system became a case study in conflict of interest, bribery, and institutionalized corruption; and our currency system criminally subverted, right under the nose of the highest court in the land, It Was:

Goodbye Representative Republic!

Hello "Dam-ocracy," Government From Hell.

The Political, Economic, and Money Systems, After the Devils Own Heart!

With the collapse of the corporate systems of finance, government, and industry; the fetters now binding our pent-up energy, will fall away, thereby allowing the second to none status now enjoyed by our military, too be duplicated within our commercial, industrial, and home grown production sectors.

Whether this occurs, or, if the system is simply, revived, and again, in expanded scope, foisted upon the worlds population, will depend upon the action, or inaction, of the productive segment of the United States citizenry.

For thousands of years the worlds productive citizens have labored in the vineyards of mankind, so to speak, only to find the products of their endeavor, priced out of their reach by the elite, often counter productive, yet controlling segment of world society.

The American citizenry (subset elites) have benefited immensely from the starvation wages for which many of our fellow human beings have toiled; pledging prodigious quantities of our future time, for items often buried in land fills; before they are even paid for.

Times, they are changing!

A new American currency is inevitable. We, the American productive class, must change the method and point at which it is introduced into the economy.

For thousands of years, the working class have been cheated out of the true value of their labor, by a system in which money is introduced from the top, enriching the law and currency manipulators.

Those producing the goods and services, were restricted to that which "trickles" down. Denial of access too significant wealth, was tantamount to denial of significant power.

The new currency must be a derivative of created wealth, not a system in which paper, reflecting nothing but the engravers art, may be traded for real wealth, as is now the case!

There is no incentive for the Law and Currency manipulators to voluntarily renounce their gravy train.

When we, the American people, wake up, and lay the proper foundation for the American Dream:

The American Century Will Have Begun!

This will not occur, until We The People, assume control of our nation, by controlling the government!

Get involved! Help this old carpenter change things.

This book and the DAM-OCRACY.NET web site, if it fulfills my hope and intent, will serve to energize the Productive Segment of our population, to not only claim our piece of the pie, but the pie itself.

Capt. John Smith at Jamestown, with his statement that "If you don't work, you don't eat," had his ducks in a row! Productive work should provide a higher standard of living, than law and currency manipulation!

ISBN 141203303-9

9 781412 033039